Chinese Responses to U.S. Military Transformation and Implications for the Department of Defense

T0306949

James C. Mulvenon, Murray Scot Tanner, Michael S. Chase,
David Frelinger, David C. Gompert, Martin C. Libicki,
Kevin L. Pollpeter

Prepared for the Office of the Secretary of Defense
Approved for public release; distribution unlimited

RAND NATIONAL DEFENSE RESEARCH INSTITUTE

The research described in this report was prepared for the Office of the Secretary of Defense (OSD). The research was conducted in the RAND National Defense Research Institute, a federally funded research and development center sponsored by the OSD, the Joint Staff, the Unified Combatant Commands, the Department of the Navy, the Marine Corps, the defense agencies, and the defense Intelligence Community under Contract DASW01-01-C-0004.

Library of Congress Cataloging-in-Publication Data is available for this publication.

ISBN 0-8330-3768-4

The RAND Corporation is a nonprofit research organization providing objective analysis and effective solutions that address the challenges facing the public and private sectors around the world. RAND's publications do not necessarily reflect the opinions of its research clients and sponsors.
RAND® is a registered trademark.

Published 2006 by the RAND Corporation
1776 Main Street, P.O. Box 2138, Santa Monica, CA 90407-2138
1200 South Hayes Street, Arlington, VA 22202-5050
201 North Craig Street, Suite 202, Pittsburgh, PA 15213-1516
RAND URL: http://www.rand.org/
To order RAND documents or to obtain additional information, contact
Distribution Services: Telephone: (310) 451-7002;
Fax: (310) 451-6915; Email: order@rand.org

Preface

Chinese strategists have avidly consumed U.S. Department of Defense writings over the past 10 years and have keenly observed the changing nature of U.S. national strategy and military transformation. Commentary by People's Liberation Army (PLA) experts on Operation Iraqi Freedom suggests that Beijing believes the Pentagon's efforts at achieving a Revolution in Military Affairs are not just succeeding, but accelerating. Yet the concomitant acceleration of the pace of Chinese military modernization also suggests that the Chinese are not dissuaded by U.S. military prowess, but instead are driven by a range of strategic and military motivations to continue their efforts apace. This report examines potential Chinese responses to U.S. transformation efforts and offers possible U.S. counterresponses. It should be of interest to analysts, warfighters, and policymakers who seek to better understand the modernization trajectory of the Chinese military, and the potential implications of PLA efforts for U.S. military capabilities in a potential China-Taiwan scenario.

This research was conducted for the Office of Force Transformation within the International Security and Defense Policy Center of the RAND National Defense Research Institute, a federally funded research and development center sponsored by the Office of the Secretary of Defense, the Joint Staff, the Unified Combatant Commands, the Department of the Navy, the Marine Corps, the defense agencies, and the defense Intelligence Community.

For more information on RAND's International Security and Defense Policy Center, contact the director, James Dobbins. He can be reached by email at dobbins@rand.org; by phone at 703-413-1100, extension 5134; or by mail at RAND Corporation, 1200 South Hayes St., Arlington, VA 22202. More information about RAND is available at www.rand.org.

Contents

Figures and Tables

Figures

Tables

Summary

Chinese strategists have avidly consumed U.S. Department of Defense (DoD) writings over the past 10 years and have keenly observed changes in U.S. national strategy and military transformation. Commentary by People's Liberation Army (PLA) experts on Operation Iraqi Freedom suggests that Beijing believes the Pentagon's efforts at achieving a Revolution in Military Affairs are not just succeeding, but accelerating. Yet the concomitant acceleration of the pace of Chinese military modernization also suggests that the Chinese are not dissuaded by U.S. military prowess, but instead are driven by a range of strategic and military motivations to continue their efforts apace. This report examines the constraints, facilitators, and potential options for Chinese responses to U.S. transformation efforts and offers possible U.S. counterresponses.

Constraints and Facilitators of Counter-Transformation Strategies

China's response to U.S. military transformation will be shaped by Beijing's key national security goals (political stability, national reunification, comprehensive national power, and rapid economic development) and the political and economic context within which the goals are pursued. Beijing's responses will be constrained by major political, social, economic, and international challenges as well as China's available package of financial and technological resources.

Defense modernization in particular must compete with several enormous, growing demands on budgetary and economic resources in a "decelerating growth" economy. Budget deficits have risen substantially since the late 1990s, and government banks are badly overextended by nonperforming loans to insolvent state factories. Rising social unrest will also heighten "national security" resource competition. Moreover, increased funding for higher education and infrastructure will be essential for defense modernization to succeed. As a result, regardless of their intrinsic strategic merit, the response options that enjoy the greatest political advantages will be those that require lower budgetary demands and start-up costs, draw upon existing technological packages, and simultaneously serve other national security goals such as internal stability and regime security.

Chinese Counter-Transformation Options

This report examines four notional Chinese response options to U.S. military transformation. Each is used as a heuristic to illustrate potentially threatening developments. Although these options are discussed in isolation, developments in China suggest that all or portions of each strategy are being pursued in earnest, and some combination of the options will likely characterize the final configuration.[1]

Option One: Conventional Modernization "Plus"

The first potential strategy is characterized by the use of conventional weapons, including space weapons, submarines, and antiship cruise missiles, to conduct anti-access operations and to strike at perceived U.S. vulnerabilities or high-value targets whose degradation, denial, or destruction could decisively influence the campaign. Of the analyzed options, this strategy is the most feasible because it relies on proven technologies that can be developed or purchased; however, it

---

[1] The use of nuclear weapons is not discussed in detail given China's lack of counterforce capabilities, but electromagnetic pulse bursts and conventional missile strikes are analyzed in Option Three.

is vulnerable to U.S. network-centric warfare (NCW) efforts. Sign-posts of Chinese efforts in this direction include increased and coordinated blue-water training by the Navy, over-water training by air units, development of long-range unmanned aerial vehicles, and development or purchase of counter-space technologies. The PLA's concentration on the use of conventional weapons against U.S. vulnerabilities indicates that the U.S. military must prepare for the PLA to seize the initiative, requiring increased attention to defensive training and technologies such as antisubmarine warfare and passive and active air base defenses.

Option Two: Subversion, Sabotage, and Information Operations
The second potential response option is based on a belief among Chinese strategists that information operations can successfully attack the two critical centers of gravity in a Taiwan scenario: the will of the Taiwanese people and U.S. military intervention. Beijing's strategy to manipulate the national psychology of the populace and leadership on Taiwan involves the full spectrum of information operations, including psychological operations, special operations, computer network operations, and intelligence operations. The goal of these efforts is to shake the widely perceived psychological fragility of the populace, causing the government to prematurely capitulate to political negotiations with the mainland. Signposts of growing PLA interest in these strategies include evidence of physical and virtual probing of Taiwanese infrastructure, greater use of regional media to send psychological-operation messages to Taiwan, and more frequent compromises of Taiwan intelligence networks on the mainland. The primary implication for the United States is that the Taiwanese side may buckle quickly, perhaps even before U.S. forces arrive, and thus any operational planning should prepare for the United States to fight alone or with only limited and possibly compromised assistance from Taiwan forces.

In terms of using information operations to affect U.S. military intervention, the use of computer network attack (CNA) to degrade or even delay a deployment of forces to Taiwan offers an attractive asymmetric strategy. Some Chinese have concluded from studies of

Desert Storm and Operation Iraqi Freedom that logistics and mobilization are a weakness of U.S. operations, particularly given their dependence on precisely coordinated transportation, communications, and logistics networks, many of which are sensitive but unclassified networks like the NIPRNET (Non-Secure Internet Protocol Router Network). PLA writings suggests that a successful CNA against these systems could have a detrimental impact on U.S. logistics support to operations and delay U.S. intervention long enough to allow the information operations and other coercion against Taiwan to have the desired effect. The advantages of this strategy are twofold: (1) it is available to the PLA in the near term, and (2) it has a reasonable level of deniability. The primary signpost of preparation for this strategy is increased evidence of probing against the NIPRNET from China-origin networks, although the nature of CNA makes attribution highly challenging. The principal implication for U.S. forces is to recognize the vulnerability of logistics and other deployment systems and to train and exercise publicly without use of the networks to diminish their value (perceived and actual) as a target.

Option Three: Missile-Centric Strategies
The third potential response is a missile-centric force that would seek to present an overwhelming short-range missile threat to Taiwan, improve China's offensive capabilities against U.S. bases in the Asia-Pacific, and give the PLA the capability to launch conventional strikes against U.S. strategic targets with conventionally armed ballistic and cruise missiles. This approach allows the Chinese to bring the fight to the full-strategic depth of the United States by attacking weak points in the enemy rear, denies the U.S. military the ability to use regional bases (Guam, for example) as sanctuaries, changes the dynamics in the early stages of a conflict, and provides an effective response to strategic attacks by American conventional forces. If the Chinese were to produce a missile-centric force designed as a counter-transformational capability, the signposts that might provide hints as to the direction of development, deployment and employment issues would include: declaratory statements, doctrinal developments, shifts in resource allocation, research and development interests, deployment

patterns and numbers, testing, and exercises. Building an effective deep attack capability is challenging from a technical standpoint, especially if the United States attempts to develop alternate strategies or force employment concepts to operate while under attack. In the end, however, the United States will be obliged to develop an approach for dealing with the threat and will need to consider a range of responses that could entail limiting its own actions, altering the basic strategy for conflict to render irrelevant the capabilities of the missile forces, employing a host of protective measures throughout its full strategic depth, or employing escalation dominance.

Option Four: Chinese Network-Centric Warfare

The fourth potential response is a Chinese version of NCW, which is likely to reflect China's strengths in operational security, operational control, surprise/stratagems, massed artillery, and rocketry. To this end, the Chinese are therefore unlikely to duplicate U.S. air power or develop doctrine on untethered operations. The major operational challenge for China vis-à-vis the United States is defeating U.S. air power, notably finding and targeting carrier battle groups (land-based air power can be countered by massed missile attacks on air bases). Massed sensors and weapons may be one way to solve this problem, but weaknesses in systems integration, logistics, and concerns over operational control of remote devices with autonomous intelligence may impede pursuit of this strategy. Signposts of a Chinese effort to develop network-centric strategies include a ramp-up in percentage of expenditures devoted to C4ISR (command, control, communications, computers, intelligence, surveillance, and reconnaissance), writings by PLA strategists and doctrinal experts espousing the idea, greater interest and resources directed toward exploiting the information technology manufacturing base, the use of smaller units in training and exercises that seem from the outside to be unusually well coordinated, and the use and coordination of an unusual number of flying objects over a large battlefield. The challenges of correctly identifying and classifying a Chinese network-centric modernization are significant, including the difficulty of signals intelligence collection against modern, encrypted, and largely fiber-optic communications systems and the smaller, component-based nature of network-centric systems.

Implications for DoD Planning, Force Transformation, and China Analysis

Implications for DoD Planning and Force Transformation

Unlike U.S. adversaries' plans in U.S. military conflicts following the end of the Cold War, China's plans have called for its forces to conduct offensive operations to seize the initiative in any Taiwan scenario, with the goal of delivering a "decisive blow" to both Taiwan and any foreign military intervention on Taiwan's behalf. As a result, DoD planning may need to focus more on defensive measures, particularly those related to protecting U.S. forward basing, satellites, information systems, and expeditionary assets, such as aircraft carriers. These efforts go well beyond simply a validation of the need for missile defense, requiring a significant reorientation of force posture, deployments, technology acquisition, and training.

What if the Chinese adopt NCW? If they do, how should the United States respond? Regardless of whether they adopt our brand of NCW, it is likely that they will enhance their investment in sensors and precision weapons. The upshot of that development is straightforward. If our NCW makes the battlefield visible to us, theirs is likely to make the battlefield visible to them. In particular, that means our own forces will be more visible to them and thus more likely to be targets. The more visible the battlefield, and the more that visibility is tantamount to destruction, the more difficult it will be to go to war with platforms. The U.S. response to that may be to accelerate certain aspects of its own NCW evolution—toward deploying sensors and weapons from a distance, or if it must operate closely, to do so either with a reduced signature (i.e., stealth) or with so much signature as to be disorienting. In either case, exposure times must be short. Both sides, China and the United States, may pursue the informatization of warfare to its logical conclusion. Victory, if not inherent in the balance of forces or unique attributes of geography, falls to whoever has the best combination of surprise, error control, fortune, and highly trained people. Ironically, a confrontation between two technologically advanced, network-centric militaries will likely reduce the importance of technology in favor of people and their ability to make rapid but accurate decisions with incomplete or overwhelming amounts of information. In such a contest, volunteer military personnel drawn from an open, educated society like that of the United States would appear to have the advantage over a stove-piped military embedded in an authoritarian state, but the blinding pace of social, cultural, and technological change in China strongly suggests that this conclusion will not always remain true.

Implications for China Analysis

The centrality of Taiwan for China's leaders makes it highly unlikely that U.S. transformation would dissuade China from devoting resources to development of capabilities it regards as essential to deter or prevent Taiwan from moving further toward formal independence (although China may be dissuaded from broader competition for military influence in the Asia-Pacific). As a result, new approaches are needed to acquire information on Chinese responses to U.S. transformation that will facilitate analysis of Chinese capabilities and intentions. Efforts require that priority be given to the recruitment and training of subject-matter experts with advanced language qualifications.

Abbreviations

C4ISR	command, control, communications, computers, intelligence, surveillance, and reconnaissance
CCP	Chinese Communist Party
CNA	computer network attack
CNE	computer network exploitation
CNO	computer network operations
CFR	Council of Foreign Relations
CONUS	continental United States
CVBG	aircraft carrier battle groups
DDOS	distributed denial of service
DoD	U.S. Department of Defense
EMP	electromagnetic pulse
GDP	gross domestic product
GNP	gross national product
GPS	Global Positioning System
ICBM	intercontinental ballistic missile
IMF	International Monetary Fund
IO	information operations
ISR	intelligence, surveillance, and reconnaissance
MOB	main operating base
NCW	network-centric warfare

NIPRNET	Non-Secure Internet Protocol Router Network
NPL	nonperforming loan
OPSEC	operational security
OTH	over-the-horizon
PAP	People's Armed Police
PGM	precision-guided munition
PLA	People's Liberation Army
PLAN	People's Liberation Army Navy
RFID	radio-frequency identification
SARS	severe acute respiratory syndrome
SOE	state-owned enterprise
SIPRI	Stockholm International Peace Research Institute
SLBM	submarine-launched ballistic missile
SRBM	short-range ballistic missile
SSBN	nuclear-powered fleet ballistic missile submarine (ship submersible ballistic nuclear)
UAV	unmanned aerial vehicle
UCAV	unmanned combat aerial vehicle

CHAPTER ONE
Introduction

Background

Chinese strategists have avidly consumed U.S. defense writings over the past 10 years and have keenly observed the changing nature of U.S. military strategy and force transformation. They have followed the emergence of networking concepts and corresponding investments. Commentary by Chinese People's Liberation Army (PLA) experts on Operation Iraqi Freedom suggests that Beijing believes the Pentagon's efforts to transform toward network-centric warfare (NCW) are not just succeeding, but accelerating. Yet the concomitant acceleration of Chinese military modernization also suggests that the Chinese are not discouraged by U.S. transformation and military victories. Although military capabilities are not China's highest priority, the U.S. Department of Defense (DoD) must assume that the Chinese will work, within their limitations, to deny the United States even greater military advantages over Chinese forces than it currently enjoys. The question is: How?

Approach

Researchers at the RAND Corporation examined China's responses to U.S. military transformation at four levels: (1) the social, political, and economic context within which Chinese priorities are set and defense decisions are made; (2) given this context and Chinese reading of U.S. military strategy, the PLA's military doctrinal and modernization options; (3) military, institutional, political, and other signposts that may provide future indications of which of the alternative military strategies China is actually pursuing; and (4) implications of alternative Chinese military strategies for DoD force planning and broader defense policies.

Context

Chinese military modernization cannot be understood in isolation. Contextual factors act as constraints, conditions, and facilitators of Chinese military strategy. On the one hand, China's astonishing economic and technological modernization since the late 1970s has been a critical facilitator of PLA modernization and strategy options. For example, the C4ISR (command, control, communications, computers, intelligence, surveillance, and reconnaissance) "revolution" in the military can be directly linked to the ability of the Chinese telecommunications market to attract foreign capital and technology, as well as the rise of an impressive, indigenous information technology sector. On the other hand, Beijing exercises strong civilian party control over the PLA, and resource allocation decisions for the military must compete with China's daunting list of domestic problems, including increasing social unrest, looming crises in the banking sector, public health (SARS and HIV/AIDS), and the environment; widening income disparity between coast and inland; increasing rural unemployment; stalled reforms of the state-owned enterprise sector; endemic official corruption; and so on. The report synthesizes existing work in these contextual areas and weighs the implications of each of key trends for military strategic choices and execution (e.g., resource levels, technology options, institutional reform).

Options

China has at least four identifiable military modernization options to counter U.S. military transformation. The first is "business as usual," focusing on conventional military modernization to achieve local deterrence, area access denial for U.S. forces, and power projection to defeat or intimidate Taiwan. Given the performance of U.S. forces in

Iraq and the pace of transformation, this option, taken alone, potentially condemns the PLA to evolving relative obsolescence. The second strategy is to develop robust information warfare (IW) capabilities to threaten broadly the vulnerabilities of U.S. NCW, including the use of computer network attack (CNA) tools to cripple rear-area logistics and communications systems necessary for U.S. deployment to a Taiwan contingency. A third strategy would be a missile-centric one that seeks to (1) present an overwhelming short-range threat to Taiwan and (2) improve China's strategic offensive threat to the United States, reasoning that U.S. apprehension about escalation may deter U.S. military intervention in defense of Taiwan or at least U.S. attacks on China itself in such a crisis. A fourth possible strategy is to ape the United States and attempt to develop NCW, at least selectively. This would require significant organizational, technological, and cultural change within the PLA. This study assesses the cost-benefit feasibility calculations, as viewed by the Chinese, for pursuing such alternative strategies (or combinations).

Signposts

While China is not likely to choose one of these alternative responses to the exclusion of the others, neither is it likely to proceed in all directions, i.e., without a central military-strategic concept. Yet it is impossible to "predict," much less "bet on," what option China will select. Therefore, it is important to look for indicators that could relate future Chinese actions with each option (or combinations), thus providing a growing appreciation over time of the path China is taking. Instead of using the term "indicators and warning," which often focuses too narrowly on intelligence collection, this study identifies "signposts," which may include broader political-military resource issues, "hardware" investments, and "software" reforms, such as joint doctrine, training, and organization, which are necessary to execute one or another of the alternatives.

Implications

The study assesses the implications of the findings from the first three sections for DoD planning, force transformation, China analysis, and other U.S. national security policies and activities. Specifically, it examines what actions the United States might take to dissuade or channel the Chinese responses. While acknowledging that U.S actions might range from changes in grand strategy and policy to force structure and operational concepts, this study focuses on implications for U.S. force capabilities.

Organization of the Report

The remainder of this report is divided into six chapters. Chapter Two examines the contextual factors shaping China's response options, including social, political, and economic factors. Chapter Three provides a methodological introduction to the report, defining network-centric warfare and explaining the typology of Chinese response options. Chapters Four through Seven outline and analyze four Chinese options (conventional modernization "plus," subversion/sabotage/information operations, missile-centric, and NCW), evaluating their feasibility and implications for U.S. forces. The appendix explores how the DoD might enhance or transcend the current transformation strategy to deal with the range of Chinese responses.

CHAPTER TWO

Contextual Factors Shaping China's Response Options

China's choice of responses to DoD transformation over the next decade will be shaped and constrained by an interplay among China's strategic goals and the political and economic context within which it pursues those goals. In this report, the term *context* refers to the most important international, political, and economic challenges that China's leaders will have to confront during the period when they are crafting their response. "Context" also includes the package of resources on which Beijing can draw in addressing these problems. This chapter focuses in particular on China's available budgetary and financial resources, as well as its technological resources.

Although these forces—national goals, policy challenges, and available resources—will not by themselves rigidly determine China's choice of responses, their impact will be very powerful. Contextual forces will

- influence the relative priority China's leaders attach to their various national security goals
- heighten political pressure to pursue some response options rather than others
- make some response options far more costly and difficult to pursue than others.

These contextual challenges will also prod China's leaders to shape or recast some to their response options in ways that allow the leadership to simultaneously address other national security goals—some of which may be unrelated to the challenge. They will also force China's leaders to confront several profound contradictions among their most basic national security goals—for example, contradictions among internal stability, economic growth, and expanding military expenditures.

Contradictory National Security Goals and Responses to U.S. Military Transformation

As China develops its response to U.S. military transformation, it will be struggling to balance four basic national security goals:

1. Ensuring the survival of the Chinese Communist Party (CCP) regime and maintaining internal stability and national unity
2. Sustaining high rates of economic growth, in particular job protection and creation, raising income levels, promoting international trade and investment, and accelerating technological modernization (Beijing views economic growth as the key "instrumental" goal—the one project that makes all of its other national security goals attainable)
3. Preventing Taiwan's permanent legal separation from China and, hopefully, eventually achieving some formal version of reunification
4. Increasing China's "comprehensive national power"—a conception of power that includes not only the expansion of Beijing's military options but also increased economic, diplomatic, political, and "soft power" influence.

When China's key national security goals are expressed in this way, as a package of general, long-term aspirations, all Chinese leaders see them as straightforward and entirely unobjectionable. But as the leadership ponders the relative priorities among these goals, the sequence in which to pursue them, and the available paths to achieve them, it must confront a number of painful short-term contradictions and trade-offs. For example, one of the riskiest trade-offs over the next decade will be the choice between the policies Beijing knows it must adopt to encourage sustained long-term economic growth and its immediate need to maintain political stability. Moreover, each of these goals will also require a significant and growing expenditure of resources, heightening the resource competition both within the broader national security sector and between security and non-security requirements.

Even where China is successful in pursuing some of its security goals, that success could generate obstacles for other security objectives. For example, Beijing clearly hopes that higher living standards and rising educational levels will strengthen the government's legitimacy. But the experience of other developing countries clearly indicates that these "human capital" improvements will also create a more assertive, restive populace that is harder to control. From the PLA's perspective, moreover, these same human capital improvements are generating the larger pool of technologically sophisticated young people it needs for any serious military modernization strategies, but they are also generating high-paying alternative non-military careers that are making recruiting and retaining technologically savvy soldiers increasingly costly and difficult.

Key National Security Goals

Regime Survival, Political Stability

For the foreseeable future, the Chinese state's central national security concern will continue to be ensuring the regime's survival and maintaining China's internal stability and national unity. As the sole surviving major Leninist power in a post-Soviet world, it is unlikely Beijing will ever be able to afford the luxury of treating internal stability as simply a "short term" or "secondary" goal. Nor can it regard internal security as something that is merely "instrumental" to other national security goals, such as increasing "comprehensive national power." The CCP leadership's attitude—captured in Deng Xiaoping's famous dictum that "stability overrides everything"—is that regime survival and internal security are central obsessions in their own right.

Beijing is most concerned about the prospects for five principal threats to internal stability:

1. The rise of any organized nationwide opposition movement or party that could offer a credible counter-elite to the CCP
2. Mass instability or protest—again, especially organized protest movements or labor unions
3. Dangerous factional divisions among the Party leadership, which Chinese leaders have historically feared (not without justification) would encourage opposition movements, protests, rebellions, or coups
4. Infiltration, subversion, and attack by the Party's perceived enemies, including not only by Taiwanese and Western agents, but also increasingly by organized underground movements such as the Falun Gong or terrorist organizations
5. Ethno-national division, particularly the rise of separatist or independence movements in China's Muslim- and Tibetan-populated borderlands (or the permanent formal separation of Taiwan).

To an enormous degree, the policies that China's leaders have been willing to adopt in pursuit of their other policy goals have been shaped and constrained by Beijing's estimate of their likely impact on internal security. For example, instability concerns have long shaped the policy sequence and pacing of China's 25-year economic and political reform movement, causing Beijing to stall or delay many industrial, financial, and legal reforms that it saw as too risky.

Increasing "Comprehensive National Power" and Military Modernization

Like the rest of Beijing's overall defense buildup, responses to U.S. military transformation will be shaped by China's desire to expand its "comprehensive national power." This concept of power, first popularized by Deng Xiaoping in the early 1980s, is a bit amorphous and is used differently by various analysts. But its essence is to denote a much broader conception of power than strictly military might. Leaders and analysts almost invariably argue that a powerful, vibrant, and technologically innovative economy forms the true cornerstone of comprehensive national power.[1] Economic power, in turn, is buttressed by the quality of a country's political and military systems, science and technology, diplomacy, and other less tangible factors.

Chinese strategic thinkers have long wrangled over the relative importance of the economic, military, diplomatic, and other components of comprehensive power and how quickly to promote each one. Most notably in the past two decades, debate has focused on how fast China should accelerate its defense buildup relative to its overall rate of economic growth. China's defense modernization and its specific responses to U.S. military transformation seem very likely to heighten this point of contention. Throughout his years as preeminent leader, Deng Xiaoping insisted that China, in its quest for comprehensive power, must focus first on laying a powerful, self-sustaining, innovative economic base. Only upon such a base could defense expenditures be increased. After Deng's passing, Jiang Zemin clung to the principle of focusing first on the economic base. But beginning in the early 1990s, a confluence of factors encouraged Beijing to accelerate defense spending. Most prominent among these were

- China's sustained rapid economic growth
- Jiang's desire to court the PLA during his succession
- the military's increased influence following its suppression of the Tiananmen protests of 1989[2]

---

[1] Implicit in this conception is a critique of what Chinese analysts regard as the one-sided, economically unsustainable pursuit of pure military might by the former Soviet Union—a mistake China hopes to avoid.

[2] There remains some disagreement among experts on the PLA as to whether or not there was an implicit "payoff" to the army for saving the Party's position in 1989, but of course, smoking-gun evidence of such a payoff is unlikely ever to be found. This analysis contends, at a minimum, that the PLA's role in 1989 dramatically reminded the Party leadership of the military's central role in regime survival and as a result very likely strengthened its political influence overall.

- China's growing recognition of rapid improvements in world military technology after the 1991 Gulf War
- Beijing's rising concern over efforts by Taiwan's last two presidents—Lee Teng-hui and Chen Shui-bian—to promote the island's independence.

The motivations for China's more concrete military development goals could be divided into "active" and "reactive" elements. Among the "active" motivations are Beijing's desire to greatly expand its options for exercising influence on its near periphery—in particular, the Taiwan Strait and South China Sea. A powerful "reactive" concern is China's fear that it is falling behind in a global competition for military modernization, a fear that was enhanced by Beijing's reading of the Gulf War in 1991 and Operation Iraqi Freedom in 2003. Chinese strategic analysts have persistently expressed concern about China's capacity to achieve its aims in a conflict in the Taiwan Strait or South China Sea—particularly in the event of U.S. intervention. To ensure its ultimate national security, China is also striving to at least maintain, and perhaps enhance, the credibility of its nuclear deterrent, as well as the coercive potential of its conventional missile forces arrayed opposite Taiwan. A particular concern is U.S. missile defense programs, which Beijing fears will eventually be extended to Taiwan.[3]

Preventing Taiwan Independence

China's goal of preventing Taiwan's permanent formal separation from the mainland, and ultimately reunifying China and Taiwan, will probably have a greater impact on Beijing's time frame for defense

---

[3] "Beijing probably assesses that U.S. efforts to develop missile defenses will challenge the credibility of China's nuclear deterrent and eventually be extended to protect Taiwan. In Beijing's view, this development would degrade the coercive value of its growing conventional ballistic-missile capability opposite the island and constitute a de facto alliance between Washington and Taipei. Beijing continues to voice opposition to missile defense, as well as concern regarding U.S. withdrawal from the Anti-Ballistic Missile Treaty. It also argues against Taiwan's inclusion in a missile defense system, albeit less stridently than in previous years." U.S. Department of Defense, *Annual Report on the Military Power of the People's Republic of China*, July 28, 2003, p. 13.

modernization than any other national security goal. Specifically, China's perception of whether or not "time is on its side" in eventually striking a reunification deal will heavily influence its sense of urgency about its military buildup. Other things being equal, the more pessimistic Beijing is that reunification can gradually be secured through peaceful negotiations and growing economic links between the mainland and Taiwan, the more likely it is to pursue a rapid buildup of its current inventory of forces, with the narrow aim of trying to prevail in a cross-Strait military engagement that it assumes will involve the United States. Over the past two decades, Beijing's assessment of cross-Strait trends has oscillated between optimism and pessimism. In the past two years, however, Taiwan President Chen Shui-bian's comments on cross-Strait relations and efforts to pass referenda first on a new constitution and later on cross-Strait security issues have caused Beijing's assessment to turn significantly more pessimistic.

Adding to the urgency of China's concerns about Taiwan independence is its fear that the Taiwan issue could also affect its prospects for maintaining regime survival, internal security, and national unity. As has been widely noted, China's post-Mao leadership has relied heavily on nationalist appeals rather than communism as a key source of legitimacy. On the one hand, China's leaders unquestionably view an eventual reunification in positive, nationalistic terms, as the crown jewel in the nation's 50-year effort to restore the territorial unity lost during the 19th and 20th centuries. CCP leaders certainly believe that a successful, peaceful reunification with Taiwan would greatly enhance their regime's domestic legitimacy. On the other hand, no Chinese leader or government could feel confident of surviving in power after the massive loss of legitimacy that would result from Taiwan achieving formal, permanent separation. Moreover, many mainlanders have voiced a visceral fear that Taiwan's independence could touch off a "domestic domino chain" of national disunity—with Taiwan's loss sparking independence movements among China's Muslims, Tibetans, or even Mongols or Koreans. Hence, Beijing desires the achievement of Taiwan's formal reunification on almost any terms—or at least the continued avoidance of its permanent formal separation—not merely for its own sake, but also because it is inextricably linked to its fears of regime collapse and national disunity. For this reason, while Beijing is probably prepared to negotiate patiently with Taiwan so long as eventual reunification seems in sight, it would likely react very strongly to any effort at formal permanent separation. But to make such a reaction credible, Beijing feels it must greatly enhance its range of military options.

Economic Modernization:
The Key Instrument—and the Key Constraint

China's leadership sees the continuation of rapid, sustained economic growth as its indispensable "instrumental" national security goal—the project that provides the resources to make all other security goals attainable. For example, in recent years, as social protests have become more common, Beijing's internal security analysts have begun abandoning the traditional Leninist theory that unrest is caused primarily by anticommunist foreign conspirators, arguing instead that sustained rapid growth, large-scale job creation, and improved social safety nets are the keys to domestic stability.[4] China's dramatic growth over the past two decades—an average annual gross domestic product (GDP) growth rate of 10.1 percent from 1980 to 1990, and 10.3 percent from 1990 to 1998—has also underwritten its rapid increase in defense expenditures since 1990.[5] The Chinese

---

[4] Indeed, there is a bit of a "magic bullet" mentality about economic development among many Chinese leaders and policy analysts. Many not only seem to assume that development will eventually cure all of China's ills but also expect that along the way to development, with each additional increment of growth, other problems will correspondingly ease. This assumption ignores or downplays a great deal of evidence from other developing countries that shows that along the way toward development, these states have encountered increases in mass instability, inequality, corruption, and many other problems—which only begin to decline at much higher levels of economic and political development. Other analysts and leaders clearly recognize that China must augment economic growth with political reforms if it is to contain unrest, but to date the top leadership has been unwilling to promote major changes and seems to find the reliance on economic growth politically easier as a response. For a discussion of this thinking, see Murray Scot Tanner, "China Rethinks Unrest," *The Washington Quarterly*, Vol. 27, No. 3, Summer 2004a, pp. 137–156.

[5] Official figures from China's State Statistical Bureau. For a discussion of alternative non-official estimates, see K. C. Yeh, "China's Economic Growth: Recent Trends and Prospects,"

government's ability not only to sustain high growth rates but also to tap into that growing social wealth and improve its capacity to develop its own military and dual-use technology will be among the most important factors determining how, and how effectively, China responds to U.S. military transformation.

Contradictions Among Beijing's Security Goals

Among the riskiest trade-offs among China's national security goals concerns the danger of political instability inherent in the policies Beijing knows it must adopt in order to sustain rapid economic growth rates. Beijing is aware that it must cut down on the inefficiencies of the old state-run economy and free up capital and other resources to accelerate the economic growth that will underwrite its other security goals. But policies toward this end run the short-term risk of greatly exacerbating unemployment, heightening financial instability, and shredding what little remains of the social safety net—all of which would probably spur further increases in mass unrest and political instability. These challenges will grow even sharper as China grapples to meet its new obligations under the World Trade Organization (WTO), which requires it to further open to foreign competition not only to its industrial sector but also to its financial and agricultural sectors. Given the centrality of regime survival and political stability among Beijing's goals, a significant increase in unrest would almost certainly lead to a major diversion of resources and capital from responses to U.S. military transformation to efforts to maintain the CCP's hold on power. At a minimum, it would probably have an impact on Beijing's specific choice of policies toward this project.

But China is already encountering increasingly daunting challenges in its effort to maintain rapid growth rates and guide

---

in Shuxun Chen and Charles Wolf, Jr., eds., *China, the United States, and the Global Economy,* Santa Monica, Calif.: RAND Corporation, MR-1300-RC, 2001, pp. 69–98 (esp. p. 72). The World Bank estimates China's 1978–1995 growth rate at 8.2 percent. Although many economists estimate that, for various methodological reasons, China's growth estimates should be lower, nearly all suggest that growth rates during this period were very high, ranging from 7 to 8.5 percent.

investment to key technological sectors. Many economists forecast that during the next decade—the period of its response to U.S. military transformation—China is most likely to face decelerating, albeit still quite solid, economic growth rates. As a result, China will have to forge a response to U.S. military transformation at a time when efforts to raise or sustain high levels of defense spending run into increasing budgetary competition and rising demands for funds to pursue other national goals. Some of these goals—most notably regime survival and internal stability—will almost certainly have a more pressing claim on leadership attention and support than efforts to respond to U.S. military transformation. Other goals—improving higher education is a key example—will have to compete for funds with military modernization in the short run, but their ultimate success is essential if most Chinese responses are to succeed.

Contextual Challenges and Constraints on Defense Modernization

Four contextual factors are likely to have the most powerful and direct impact on China's overall military buildup and its response options to U.S. military transformation:

1. China's perception of the trend in cross-Strait relations, which it currently believes is deteriorating
2. Stiffening competition for financial and budgetary resources in a decelerating growth economy
3. The increasing challenges and national security "opportunity costs" of maintaining internal stability and the regime's hold on power
4. China's improving but unevenly expanding technological base.

Trends in Cross-Strait Relations

Almost certainly, the most powerful "international"[6] contextual factor shaping Beijing's choice of defense modernization strategies will be its assessment of the long-term prospects for achieving its goals in cross-Strait relations. In the past year, China's perception of the trends for formal reunification with Taiwan has deteriorated from moderate optimism toward greater pessimism in response to recent statements and proposals by Taiwan President Chen Shui-bian. Chen's pledge in his 2000 inaugural address not to take any of five specific measures that might be perceived as trying to establish Taiwan's independence initially heartened Beijing. But in Beijing's eyes, many of Chen's subsequent actions—his characterization of mainland China and Taiwan as "two states, one on either side of the straits," his call for constitutional reforms that could redefine Taiwan into formal independence, and his efforts during the 2004 election campaign to promote referenda that Beijing perceives as part of a gradual strategy toward formal independence—have virtually destroyed his credibility as a potential interlocutor in reunification negotiations. While most observers agree that as early as 1995–1999, China had already resolved to accelerate its efforts to build up the necessary forces to compel Taiwan to negotiate reunification, Western analysts who have had contact with Chinese officials report that Chen's recent moves and his narrow reelection have heightened Beijing's sense of urgency. Thus, China's military modernization during the period of its response to U.S. military transformation will be driven in large measure by a desire to acquire quickly the best possible mixture of economic-diplomatic carrots and military sticks sufficient to reassert the credibility of its military threat and deter or prevent Taiwan from achieving permanent formal separation. Ultimately, Beijing hopes such an influence package will prod the island's leaders into returning to the long-term negotiating process of the early 1990s under some vague version of the "one China principle." In other words, whatever

---

[6] Because Beijing considers Taiwan to be an inalienable part of China, it of course does not consider its relations with Taipei to be a matter of "international" relations.

the actual political relations between the two sides, formally there is but one China of which Taiwan is an inalienable part.

Stiffening Competition for Financial and Budgetary Resources

The desire of the Chinese leadership—especially the PLA leadership —to expand its resources available for military modernization and a possible confrontation with Taiwan will run up against several serious domestic challenges that are already dramatically heightening the political competition for budgetary and financial resources. While it is relatively easy to identify the factors that might produce slower economic growth and tighter budgetary competition, it is far more difficult to forecast with any precision the impact these forces will have on the defense funding burden that the Chinese government might be willing or able to carry. The reasons for this difficulty are methodological, economic, and political:

- First, forecasting future defense spending founders methodologically on the vast differences among the estimates of total Chinese defense spending put forward by non-Chinese experts. While all experts agree that real defense spending greatly exceeds the officially announced military budget (about US$22.4 billion in 2003), estimates of actual spending vary significantly, depending on the assumptions and methods employed.[7]
- Second, even if estimates could be agreed upon, it would still be difficult to estimate China's economic "bearing capacity" for defense expenditure and how this might limit future spending.
- Finally, the question of how much China is willing to devote to defense modernization is ultimately a political decision that the leadership must make while weighing the pressures and opportunity costs of defense spending versus competing social needs.

---

[7] Range of estimates, as well as a discussion of the problems of estimation, taken from Keith Crane, Roger Cliff, Evan S. Medeiros, James C. Mulvenon, and William H. Overholt, *Modernizing China's Military: Economic Opportunities and Constraints*, unpublished RAND research, 2004.

This last decisive factor is probably the most difficult for foreign analysts to estimate.

Establishing the Baseline: China's Current Defense Burden. To provide a general picture of the increasing competition for budgetary and financial resources within which the PLA must operate, this section first establishes a baseline of the Chinese defense sector's current claim on resources and then examines the future trends in available resources and the other competing social claims. Although several major studies of China's defense system confidently assert various forecasts of China's future capacity to sustain recent high levels of defense expenditure, these assertions must be treated with great caution.[8] Most provide no explicit assumptions or analysis concerning China's prospective economic growth rates, its major competing budgetary needs, or the magnitude of China's "defense burden" (e.g., defense spending as a percentage of GDP) relative to other countries.

A cursory examination of the increases in official Chinese defense spending since 1990—characterized by persistent double-digit annual increases—can leave the misleading impression that resource limitations and budgetary competition are simply not a significant problem for the PLA. But the available data on Chinese budgetary priorities and allocations make evident that over the past 25 years defense modernization has had to compete politically with

---

[8] According to DoD's annual report on Chinese military power, "Estimates of total spending range from $45 billion to $65 billion; annual spending could increase in real terms three- to four-fold by 2020" (Introduction, p. 5), and later, "Projecting Chinese defense spending over a long period of time is problematic... However, anticipated economic growth would define somewhat the boundaries of future defense expenditures. Using this method, annual defense spending could increase in real term three- to four-fold between now and 2020" (p. 42). The report does not identify what growth rate is anticipated or the bases for that forecast. The Council on Foreign Relations task force reports that "in spite of China's impressive growth rate in military spending over recent years, the likelihood of ever-increasing demands for government funding in areas other than military development will constrain its pace of modernization in the long term" (p. 7), and later, "the Task Force concludes that spending on force modernization and equipment purchases at approximately the rate seen in recent years is unlikely to cause unacceptable budget shortages for the next three to five years. A decline in defense spending is especially unlikely during this time period unless China's leaders conclude they have acquired the necessary capabilities vis-à-vis Taiwan" (p. 59).

other national security and non-security related priorities and has not always come up the clear winner. Moreover, tightening economic, budgetary, and financial trends all point to the conclusion that during the next decade the competition among national defense and other priorities will sharpen substantially—all in the context of a long-term deceleration in economic growth punctuated by short cycles of boom and downturn. Beijing's leaders, moreover, are likely to view many other budgetary priorities as far more immediate and pressing than programs designed as a response to U.S. military transformation.

An examination of several mainstream estimates of real Chinese defense spending suggests that China is already carrying a defense burden that is moderate to high, but comparable to other major military powers in the East Asia region. This study draws on official Chinese 2003 defense budget figures, as well as estimates by RAND specialists, an expert task force organized by the Council of Foreign Relations (CFR), and DoD's annual report on China's military (see Table 2.1). Not surprisingly, the lowest of these is the official Chinese budgetary figure, which yields an estimate of 1.81 percent of GDP. Based on a detailed calculation drawn from previously unexploited official sources, the lead author of this report generates budgetary figures that suggest defense burden estimates of 2.44 to 3.09 percent. Higher estimates range from 3.58 percent (CFR [low estimate]) to 5.28–5.45 percent (DoD and CFR [high estimate]). Since there are numerous methodological problems in using some of these estimates to calculate defense burdens based on the dollar value of China's GDP, they are used here only to give a rough estimate.

The lower nonofficial estimates (which range from 2.5 to 3.0 percent of GDP), if accurate, would imply that China's defense burden is significantly higher than those of several other regional powers (e.g., Japan, Indonesia), equivalent to others (e.g., Taiwan, South Korea, India, the United States), but lower than others (e.g., Pakistan).[9] The highest of these estimates (ranging from 5.2 to 5.5 per-

---

[9] All comparative data are from the Stockholm International Peace Research Institute (SIPRI), SIPRI Facts on International Relations and Security Trends, Military Expenditure Database. Unless otherwise stated, all data are from 2001. Concerning the source of its data,

cent of GDP), if accurate, would imply that China is currently devoting a significantly higher percentage of its GDP to military spending than that *officially reported* by most other major powers in Asia (see Table 2.2). But even the higher estimates, though substantial, are quite comparable to the defense burdens borne by many of these other regional powers at various times in the past 15 years, particularly in the latter years of the Cold War.[10] Perhaps more importantly, none of these estimates of China's defense burden even approaches the debilitating levels of military spending borne by the former Soviet Union in its final years (estimated at 15.8 percent of GDP in 1988). This last point reflects Deng Xiaoping's firm insistence that defense spending should only grow on the basis of a strong, stable economy.[11]

Table 2.1
Ranges of Chinese Defense Budget Estimates

Estimate	Defense Burden (Percentage of GDP)
Official Chinese Defense Budget	1.81
RAND (Mulvenon) estimate	2.44–3.09
Department of Defense	5.28
Council on Foreign Relations	3.58–5.45

SIPRI notes that its "military expenditure data are entirely based on open sources, and as much as possible on official data."

[10] Taiwan, for example, reported official defense spending that implied a defense burden of 5.0 to 5.1 percent annually from 1988 to 1990; South Korea's official defense burden in the late 1980s was 4.1 to 4.2 percent; Pakistan's official defense burden in was 6.0 to 6.2 percent from 1988 to 1989; and the United States declined from 5.7 to 4.1 percent from 1988 to 1994. It should be noted that all nonofficial estimates of Chinese defense spending used here assume significant concealment of spending by China, but the SIPRI comparative data rely primarily on open, official sources. We cannot rule out that data for some of these countries during these periods could also reflect significant concealment and therefore understate defense spending and burdens. Comparative data from SIPRI Facts on International Relations and Security Trends, Military Expenditure Database.

[11] Given its 2003 GDP of US$1.23 trillion, a defense burden of 15.8 percent would imply a defense budget in excess of US$194 billion, which is nearly 25 percent higher than even the highest purchasing power parity estimate of Chinese defense spending reported in Crane (2003) and more than twice the second highest estimate.

Table 2.2
Ranges of Defense Budgets Among Asian Countries

Other Powers in Asia	2001 Defense Burden (Percentage of GDP)
Japan	1.0
Indonesia	1.1
China (official)	1.81
India	2.5
Taiwan	2.6
South Korea	2.8
United States	3.1
Russia	3.8
Pakistan	4.5
USSR (1988)	15.8

SOURCE: Stockholm International Peace Research Institute, using official budget figures.

China's defense sector has not always been a political winner in recent budgetary competitions. Defense spending as a share of China's total official budget has dropped significantly since 1978—from 15 to 8 percent. And while defense's share did trend upward a bit during the early 1990s—from 8 to 10 percent—since 1998 it has fluctuated between 7 and 8 percent. Defense spending as a share of the total official budget has been lagging several other categories of expenditures, most notably social and educational expenses, and money spent on government administration (see Figure 2.1).

Calls to Increase Military Spending. There is already evidence that tighter budgets are leading some within the PLA to step up the political pressure for an increased slice of this more slowly growing pie. The consensus originally established by Deng Xiaoping and Jiang Zemin—that China must first establish a strong, vibrant economy, and only on that basis raise military expenditures—show signs of fraying around the edges. At least a few PLA officers have begun to argue more overtly that after nearly a quarter century of reform and rapid growth, it is time to accelerate military spending even more. In spring 2003, for example, several military delegates at the annual

Figure 2.1
Chinese Budget Categories, 1978–2003

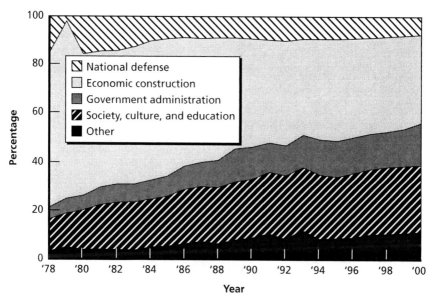

RAND *MG340-2.1*

session of the National People's Congress—China's legislature—publicly and frankly suggested that the official 9.6 percent annual increase in funding for the PLA was not sufficient. Many argued that an economic power as great as China needed to strengthen its military even faster, while others contended that without a more powerful military the economic base of China's comprehensive national power could not be protected.[12]

Such calls have not yet emerged from the top Party leadership, however, nor do they appear to be playing a role in China's ongoing succession to its "fourth generation" leadership—at least not yet.

---

[12] James Mulvenon, "Party-Army Relations Since the 16th Party Congress: The Battle of the 'Two Centers'?" in Andrew Scobell and Larry Wortzel, eds., *Civil-Military Change in China: Elites, Institutes, and Ideas After the 16th Party Congress*, Carlisle, Pa.: U.S. Army War College, Strategic Studies Institute, 2004, pp. 11–48.

Despite his apparent disagreement with Jiang on several other issues, General Secretary Hu Jintao, Jiang's designated successor, has thus far publicly echoed the line long established by Deng and Jiang. Although Hu has called for improvements by "leaps and bounds" in military modernization, he has also insisted that the rapid development of China's overall economy must remain the Party's central focus, and the key conditioning factor for how fast defense spending can increase.[13]

A More Slowly Growing Pie: Challenges to Sustained Rapid Economic Growth. Whether defense spending accounts for 1.8 percent or 5.0 percent of GDP, China's ability to funnel additional money, in real terms, to the defense sector will depend largely on the Chinese economy's capacity to continue generating relatively high rates of economic growth with relatively low inflation rates. But China is already encountering increasingly daunting challenges in its effort to maintain rapid growth rates and guide investment to key technological sectors. Many experts on China's economy estimate that over the next decade, China will probably be able to sustain moderately high average growth rates—estimates of average GDP growth rate typically range between 4 percent and 8 percent, clustering around 6.5 percent—but it will have great difficulty resuming and sustaining the historic double-digit rates of the 1980s and 1990s.[14] Deceleration began even before the 1997–1999 Asian financial crisis, with China's GDP growth rate slowing from its torrid 10 to 14 percent annual pace of 1992–1995. By 1999, when the financial crisis undercut both China's regional export markets and its

---

[13] Murray Scot Tanner, "Hu Jintao as China's Emerging National Security Leader," in Andrew Scobell and Larry Wortzel, eds., *Civil-Military Change in China: Elites, Institutes, and Ideas After the 16th Party Congress*, Carlisle, Pa.: U.S. Army War College, Strategic Studies Institute, 2004b, pp. 49–76; see also Mulvenon (2004).

[14] For a detailed analysis of several alternative forecasts, see K. C. Yeh, "China's Economic Growth: Recent Trends and Prospects," in Shuxun Chen and Charles Wolf, Jr., eds., *China, the United States, and the Global Economy*, Santa Monica, Calif.: RAND Corporation, MR-1300-RC, 2001, pp. 69–98 (esp. pp. 82–92). Yeh himself provides projections ranging from 3.8 to 6.9 percent, depending primarily on China's future savings rate and total factor productivity growth.

sources of foreign direct investment, the officially reported growth rate had slowed to 7.1 percent. Several experienced Western experts on the Chinese economy have closely examined these figures and believe the actual rate was closer to 5.5 percent or lower.[15] China's economic deceleration also may not follow a steady path, but rather one punctuated by alternating short-term boomlets and downturns. China's official 2003 growth rate of 9.1 percent, for example, has been characterized by official economists as "overheating" brought on in part by excessive government bond issues, and their announced target for 2004 is a more moderate 7 percent growth rate.

While a detailed analysis of China's future growth prospects is beyond the focus of this study, there is strong consensus among economists that China will likely be able to call on several important sources to sustain fairly high growth rates. These include continued technological improvements and a large, increasingly educated, inexpensive, and mostly well-controlled labor pool. China is also able to draw on very large capital flows from direct foreign investment, as well as extremely high rates of household savings (around 40 percent), most of which is saved in state-owned banks.[16]

But China will have difficulty sustaining many of these growth factors at their current levels. The recent rise in foreign investment inflows could slow, either temporarily or for a sustained period, as a result of a number of reasonably high probability factors. These could include growing international investor concern about political instability, social unrest, continued corruption scandals, financial system insolvency, continued currency inconvertibility, slow Chinese compliance with economic and legal commitments under WTO, or even the rise of more attractive alternative investment venues.[17] Acting singly, each of these factors could have a significant impact on foreign investment. But given the interconnection that many of these pro-

---

[15] "Special Report: Truth or Consequences: China's GDP Numbers," *China Economic Quarterly*, Vol. 8, No. 1, First Quarter 2003, pp. 32–41.

[16] Yeh (2001), pp. 73–81.

[17] Charles Wolf, Jr., et al., *Fault Lines in China's Economic Terrain*, Santa Monica, Calif.: RAND Corporation, MR-1686-NA/SRF, 2003, pp. 143–151.

spective problems have to China's chronic problems of weak state discipline and legality, they are more likely to occur in clusters, potentially heightening their impact. High household savings rates in state banks are very likely to be eroded by reforms that are privatizing many key social expenditures—health care, pensions, housing— forcing citizens to dip into their own resources for these services. An increasingly unfavorable ratio of current workers to retirees and the gradual emergence under WTO of alternative savings and investment opportunities for average Chinese workers are also likely to cut into the vast pool of state bank savings available for government investment.[18] Growing calls for protectionism from China's trade partners may slow China's exports, which now equal about one-fifth of GDP. And even though the gradual dismantling of the state-owned enterprise system and the shift of many peasants out of agricultural work are freeing up vast pools of cheap, unemployed labor, it is unclear whether most of these persons have suitable skills to contribute to the new economy or will instead become a burden on the economy.[19]

In sum, there is good reason to believe that China's near-term defense modernization will be based in an economy facing declining, albeit still quite solid, growth rates. The rates forecast by many economists would permit China to sustain very significant increases in defense spending. But if average growth rates decline by several percentage points in years to come, then a continuation of the type of double-digit annual increases in official defense spending that China bore during the 1990s would imply a rapidly growing overall defense burden on the economy. This increased defense burden would occur at the same time that China is facing growing demands from a variety of sectors that are essential to its other long-term national security goals.

---

[18] Yeh (2001), pp. 81–85.

[19] Dorothy Solinger, on the basis of extensive interviews with new urban unemployed, argues that the vast majority of these workers are not suited for work in emerging manufacturing or service industries. See Dorothy Solinger, "State and Society in Urban China in the Wake of the 16th Party Congress," *China Quarterly*, Vol. 176, December 2003, pp. 943–959. For a more optimistic assessment of these workers, see Yeh (2001), pp. 85–86.

Pressure from Growing Fiscal Challenges. China's available range of options for defense modernization will also be constrained by an increasingly tight budget and growing demands—both security related and non-security related—on central government coffers. Since the late 1990s, China has faced a gradual increase in its official budget deficit. Historically, China's official budget deficits have usually constituted a rather low percentage of GDP and by 1996 had fallen to around 1.5 percent.[20] However, with the late 1990s economic slowdown, the deficit spiked to 4 percent of GDP in 1999. The deficit is now hovering in the range of 3 to 3.5 percent of GDP and, in absolute terms, has reached record levels. From the late 1990s to 2003, much of this rising deficit was traceable to the government's heavy reliance on state investments in fixed assets to keep official growth rates up around 8 percent.[21] International Monetary Fund (IMF) economists estimate that as a result, China's official accumulated debt stock had reached 23 percent of GDP by the end of 2000 and has risen since then.[22] While economists differ in their assessments of the seriousness of such deficit rates, some Chinese state economists have publicly described the 3 percent mark as "an internationally recognized alarm level."[23] Regardless, the growing budget

---

[20] Raju Jan Singh, "China's Medium-Term Fiscal Challenges," in International Monetary Fund, *IMF World Economic Outlook: Recessions and Recoveries*, Washington, D.C., April 2002, pp. 36–37.

[21] The deficit is officially estimated at RMB309.8 billion for 2002 and RMB319.8 billion for 2003. According to Asian Development Bank sources, China's Ministry of Finance estimates that fixed asset expenditures have been responsible for a significant portion of China's growth rate—between 1.5 and 2 percentage points—every year from 1998 to at least 2002. James Kynge, "Rural Poverty May Threaten China's Future, Zhu Warns National People Congress," *Financial Times*, March 6, 2003, p. 11; Joseph Kahn, "China Gambles on Big Projects for Its Stability," *New York Times*, January 13, 2003a; "Provincial Puzzle," *China Economic Review*, April 2003; "Special Report: Truth or Consequences: China's GDP Numbers," *China Economic Quarterly*, Vol. 8, No. 1, First Quarter 2003, pp. 32–41; "People's Republic of China," in Asian Development Bank, *Asian Development Outlook 2003*, Hong Kong: Oxford University Press, 2003.

[22] Singh (2002).

[23] "China Advised to Keep an Eye on Fiscal Deficit," *People's Daily Online*, December 27, 2002. For an example of a more sanguine assessment by an IMF economist, see Singh (2002).

deficit places greater pressure on other government expenditures, including those required for strategies to counter U.S. military transformation.[24]

But China's official budget deficit barely scrapes the surface of the financial challenges the government is facing; indeed, some of China's most serious financial burdens have increasingly been taken off the official budget in the past two decades. By far, the most serious dilemma concerns the costs of propping up China's chronically inefficient state-owned enterprises (SOEs), which even after 25 years of market-oriented reform still officially number over 159,000 and employ more than 74 million workers.[25] Here in particular, the specter of unrest indirectly distorts government policies essential to reform and long-term growth. Throughout the late 1980s and 1990s, Beijing delayed fundamental enterprise and banking reforms, while the official budgets of these enterprises were steadily removed from the central government's budget and financed instead by loans drawn on China's major state-owned banks. But with unprofitable enterprises unable to repay, a great number of these loans—several Chinese and foreign economists estimate perhaps 50 percent—are now, in reality, nonperforming. Although some analysts contend that technically these banks debts are no longer the legal liability of the Chinese central government, Beijing certainly could not sit idly by as these key financial institutions went bankrupt, with all the attendant financial chaos, investor panic, rising unemployment, and political unrest that would almost certainly ensue.

Although Chinese authorities have undertaken numerous reforms to tighten up these banks' lending practices, the overwhelming consensus of economists is that these policies have not been very effective, and banks are still subject to heavy pressure from central and local governments to loan money to un-creditworthy enterprises

---

[24] "People's Republic of China" (2003).

[25] State Statistical Bureau, *China Statistical Yearbook 2002*, Beijing: China Statistics Press, 2002, Table 5-7, p. 126. See also Philip P. Pan, "China Accelerates Privatization, Continuing Shift from Doctrine," *Washington Post*, November 12, 2003, p. A14.

and projects.[26] Inevitably, the banks have accumulated mounting nonperforming loans (NPLs) on their balances sheets. In January 2001, after years of public denials, the Bank of China officially estimated that these NPLs account for about 25 percent of all outstanding loans, which is also equal to about a quarter of China's GDP.[27] This figure, if correct, is approximately equal to the ratio of bad loans in Japan and South Korea on the eve of the 1997 financial crisis. But independent economists, both Chinese and Western, feel certain that the actual figure is far higher, with estimates ranging from 33 to 53 percent or even 60 percent of GDP as of the late 1990s.[28]

When these nonperforming state bank loans are added to China's accumulated debt stock from successive years of deficit spending, the IMF estimates China's total public debt as of 2000 at between 75 and 100 percent of China's entire GDP—a ratio that is probably still growing.[29] By comparison, it was noted earlier that China's 2003 defense expenditures probably accounted for somewhere between 1.8 and 5.5 percent of GDP.

In recent years, Western experts on the Chinese economy have laid out several scenarios—some more plausible, some less so—under

---

[26] Before 1998, the People's Bank of China (PBC)—China's Central Bank—was organized with a central branch and branches in each of China's 31 provinces and over 2,000 counties, each of which was under the direct leadership of Party and government officials at that level, not superior-level PBC officials. Although a 1998 reorganization into one central and nine regional banks was intended to strengthen bank independence, local officials still retain tremendous administrative, economic, and personal control over bank staff in their area. Wolf et al. (2003), pp. 120–127.

[27] Wolf et al. (2003), p. 125; Thomas J. Christensen, "China," in Richard J. Ellings and Aaron J. Friedberg, eds., *Strategic Asia 2002–2003: Asian Aftershocks*, Seattle: National Bureau of Asian Research, 2002, p. 76.

[28] In a striking admission of how badly officials are understating the problem, the official *People's Daily* on January 27, 2003, reported on its Web site that a Goldman-Sachs economist estimated China's banks would require a US$290 billion bailout—flatly contradicting a claim made in another official Chinese financial paper that the bailout might cost only US$40 billion. See "China Bank Bailout Could Need US$290 Bln: Report," *People's Daily Online*, January 27, 2003.

[29] Many economists believe, for example, that not only are the absolute number of bad loans continuing to increase but also the ratio of bad loans, because banks remain under pressure to keep SOEs afloat and "often roll over the bad loans, so they do not show on their balance sheets" (Wolf et al., 2003, p. 125). See also Singh (2002).

which China's growing fiscal crisis could upset or undermine the sustained, high-level economic growth on which China's defense modernization relies. The more dramatic of these scenarios involve panics and bank runs by depositors who suddenly lose faith in the government's banks.[30] But a more certain and more subtle impact is the financial system's "drag" on economic growth and technological modernization. State bank loans to SOEs eat up more than 80 percent of all state bank lending, one of the two major sources of the capital on which many economists believe China's rapid growth has depended. One recent RAND study summarized bluntly the effect on growth:

> Even if no crisis occurs, the process could drain the banks' loanable resources, because lending to the SOEs is a one-way flow of funds into a bottomless pit.[31]

As a result, "the banks' capacity to support healthy projects could thus be greatly reduced, restricting the growth of investment."[32] Therefore, for the foreseeable future, the drain on capital and the fiscal pressure seem likely to continue.

Other Competing Resource Demands. In the decade to come, Beijing will face increasingly pressing demands for social spending that will vie with the needs of defense modernization in the short term. Many of these nonmilitary projects—most notably education and infrastructure—must be funded if Beijing wishes to sustain economic growth, eliminate bottlenecks, and lay a solid social foundation for long-run defense modernization. Other priorities, such as pensions and health care, must be met to maintain social stability at a

---

[30] A thoughtfully researched review of these scenarios is Wolf et al. (2003), pp. 135–139. See also Nicholas R. Lardy, "Sources of Macroeconomic Instability in China," in David L. Shambaugh, ed., *Is China Unstable? Assessing the Factors*, Armonk, New York: M. E. Sharpe, 2000, pp. 57–62, and Peter Bottelier, "How Stable Is China? An Economic Perspective," in Shambaugh (2000), pp. 63–78.

[31] Wolf et al. (2003), pp. 135–139.

[32] Wolf et al. (2003), p. 138. See also Andy Xie, "Why High-Speed Growth Won't Solve China's Financial Problems," *SCMP.com*, January 27, 2003.

level that would permit Beijing to focus its national security budget on technical modernization rather than fighting unrest. Among the most pressing future nonmilitary demands are:

- **Higher Education.** For China to train the personnel necessary for the more technologically advanced response options to U.S. military transformation, it must greatly expand both high school and four-year college-equivalent education. At present, China's basic literacy rate and elementary school graduation rates are rather high compared with other countries at the same level of development, but its high school and college graduation rates lag considerably. Finally, as many observers have noted, the increasingly profitable alternative careers available to Chinese students who possess such scarce scientific and technological talents—both in China and abroad—are creating major problems for the PLA in recruiting and retaining talented officers. Efforts to bring these officers' pay even close to market alternatives would further heighten the PLA's budgetary challenges.[33]
- **Health Care.** China has witnessed a virtual collapse of it former socialist health care system, particularly the loss of affordable access by peasants and laid-off state enterprise workers, who relied on their former work units for coverage. The advent of SARS, AIDS, and other epidemic diseases raises the specter of extremely expensive potential health threats that could create sudden added budgetary challenges for the central government.

---

[33] Roger Cliff, *The Military Potential of China's Commercial Technology*, Santa Monica, Calif.: RAND Corporation, MR-1292-AF, 2001 (esp. pp. 37–41); "The PLA is also likely to face other economic and educational bottlenecks, especially in labor markets, i.e., the low educational level of peasant soldiers and the need to compete with the growing private sector for college-educated and noncommissioned officers." Harold Brown, Joseph W. Prueher, and Adam Segal, *Chinese Military Power*, New York: Council on Foreign Relations, 2003, p. 59. One expert has argued that the PLA's recruitment and retention problems may be even greater than those faced by the militaries of the United States and other developed countries because "...the gap between the old economy and the new in terms of pay, lifestyle, and prestige [and, one could add, opportunities for travel to the West] is likely to make the private sector in high-tech very desirable for young Chinese elites" (Christensen, 2002, p. 47).

The failure to revive the public health system could also become a chronic drag on economic growth.

- **Pensions for State Workers.** The withholding of pensions owed to retired state enterprise and government workers by insolvent work units is one of the most powerful and widespread causes of protest in China today, according to official police sources.[34] In response, governments at all levels have often been forced to pay out large lump-sum back payments—a sudden and unpredictable budgetary burden. China's age demographics are deteriorating, moreover, causing the number of current workers per pension recipient to decrease.

- **Environmental Protection and Resource Shortages.** Economists note China's increasing dependence on imported sources of energy, in particular petroleum.[35] In the past two decades, China has also had to wrestle with a increasing shortage of freshwater, particularly in many of the fast-growing urban centers of north and east China.

- **Infrastructure Improvements.** China's overburdened and crumbling transportation system is becoming an increasingly serious bottleneck for growth. Investment in railroads has lagged far behind the construction of new highways, causing slowdowns in deliveries of key commodities, such as the coal supplies from the northwestern producer provinces on which coastal factories and power plants rely. The result has been increasing brownouts and interruptions in production. Backlogs at seaports have also caused significant delays and increases in transport prices, which are fueling inflation.[36]

---

[34] Tanner (2004a).

[35] Erica Strecker Downs, *China's Quest for Energy Security*, Santa Monica, Calif.: RAND Corporation, MR-1244-AF, 2000.

[36] Keith Bradsher, "A Logjam for Transportation in China," *New York Times*, March 5, 2004.

Political Instability as an "Opportunity Cost" on National Security

During the period when the Beijing leadership crafts its response to U.S. military transformation, its most pressing national security concern will probably be increased political instability. For several years after the suppression of the urban protests and the Tibetan uprising of 1989, the government faced little documented unrest. But Chinese security sources indicate that social unrest began rising steadily again beginning in the early to mid-1990s, accelerating dramatically with the economic downturn of 1997–1999, and continuing a steady climb even as the economy has recovered. Between 1993 and 2003, incidents of mass protest—sit-ins, strikes, marches, roadblocks, even riots—expanded by more than six times from 8,700 to over 58,000, according to official estimates from the Ministry of Public Security.[37] The economically depressed northeastern rustbelt bordering Russia and North Korea has been hammered especially hard, with officially reported protests numbering in the thousands annually. Protests are also growing rapidly in their size, level of organization, and tactical sophistication.

Although unrest has not yet approached levels where it directly threatens either the Party's grip on power or China's national unity, these prospects cannot be ruled out in the decade to come. As demonstrated by the 1989 Tiananmen protests and the wave of unrest in 1997–1999, protest levels have sometimes "spiked" suddenly to very dangerous levels in response to major economic downturns, inflation, widespread anger over corruption, and other crises. Rising unrest has contributed to increasingly serious problems of governability in China, and it is quite reasonable to assume that the state will face at least one or more major social order threats to its leadership during the period when it is trying to respond to U.S. military transformation.

The rise in unrest will affect Beijing's response to U.S. military transformation in several ways. Most importantly, it constitutes a growing "opportunity cost" within China's broader expenditure on

---

[37] Tanner (2004a).

national security. Specifically, Beijing must devote a rising share of resources to developing larger internal security forces and adopting security equipment and strategies that are far more sophisticated—and far more expensive—than the simple brute force repression employed in Tiananmen and Tibet in the late 1980s. China's regular police force has doubled in size in the past 15 years, from around 800,000 to 1.7 million, while the paramilitary People's Armed Police (PAP) force has also been expanded to over 1 million. Police antiriot units that historically relied on raw numbers, muscle power, nightsticks, moderate amounts of teargas, and periodic live-fire now require increased funding for more sophisticated anti-demonstration training and modern nonlethal crowd control equipment. To ensure loyalty, the central government and many localities may also be forced to increase salaries of the regular police and PAP. They also continue to raise wages for the PLA—still the ultimate guarantor of the Party's power if the police fail.

Moreover, police leaders increasingly insist that repression alone is not sufficient to contain unrest, because its roots ultimately lie in economic and social problems such as layoffs, unpaid pensions and health benefits, widening income gaps, excessive tax burdens on farmers, and official corruption and abuses. Fearful that even greater unrest could result from bankrupting more SOEs, national and local officials are pressuring banks to carry ever-larger numbers of bad loans to buck up these SOEs. Increasingly, local governments have also chosen to ante-up emergency payments to pacify strikes and protests by workers and pensioners. There is no way to estimate the amount of these buy-offs. But a number of economic and security officials fear that the demand for such payouts could grow worse because they are already provoking a costly "bidding war" among disgruntled citizens, demonstrating that "protest pays" and encouraging more and more workers to take their demands to the streets. As a result, unrest, or more specifically the CCP's efforts to avert it, constitutes an increasing drag on the economic growth on which China's U.S. military transformation response strategies will be built.

China's Militarily Relevant Technology Base

Just as China's tightening financial climate will set the limits on the resources China can commit to defense modernization, the packages of militarily significant technologies available to Beijing over the next decade will shape its response options to U.S. military transformation. Although China's defense science and technology sector has in recent years finally begun to show real signs of life after decades of slow progress, "China's current military technology...is still largely based on 1950s-era Soviet technology." A recent CFR study of China's defense modernization summarized several of the key obstacles to defense technological modernization:

> China's abilities to develop, produce, and, most important, integrate indigenously sophisticated military systems are limited. China is advancing less rapidly in developing military technology than in the application of certain commercial technologies because the system of innovation and acquisition, unlike in the civilian economy, remains the province of the PLA, the defense establishment bureaucracy, and state-owned enterprises whose productivity has lagged behind their nonmilitary and non–state-owned counterparts.[38]

The tightening competition for budgetary and financial resources will continue to put pressure on efforts to revive the defense science and technology sector and will also place limits on China's capacity to continue importing key military technologies from Russia and other suppliers. Of course, any downturn in relations with key suppliers, especially a reversal in China's recent unusually good relations with Russia, would further exacerbate these supply challenges.[39]

---

[38] Brown, Prueher, and Segal (2003), p. 6.

[39] "Among China's other external relations, its relationship with Russia is the one most likely to influence the pace and scope of Chinese military modernization. China is critically dependent on Russia for more advanced weapons and defense technologies as well as spare parts and repairs. Suspicion by either side of the other's strategic intentions could derail the relationship. Since this supply relationship is a significant vulnerability for the Chinese, China would like to reduce its dependence on Russia, although the poor state of China's own defense industries remains a significant impediment to achieving this goal." Brown, Prueher, and Segal (2003), p. 34.

As a result of these pressures, China has in recent years increasingly turned to its rapidly expanding domestic civilian technology base to support its defense modernization strategies. These civilian industries enjoy a major advantage over defense industries in gaining access to state-of-the-art or near state-of-the-art international components, equipment, and processes. In the long run, diffusion of technology from China's most successful of these civilian technology sectors will probably prove to be the most promising source of technology for China's defense modernization.[40]

A recent analysis of the potential of China's commercial technology sector to support military modernization found very uneven progress among eight major technology sectors with the highest capacity for military application.[41] Among the most noteworthy:

- China's most advanced microelectronics facilities were six to eight years behind the late 1990s' state of the art—virtually halving China's gap behind world standards a decade earlier—and at current rates of progress could catch up by around 2008. But its most advanced facilities are still very few in number and highly reliant on imported equipment. As of the late 1990s, China's most advanced integrated circuit joint ventures were using 6-inch, 0.8-micron technology to produce 4-Mb DRAM chips, with plans for projects that would soon introduce 0.5-micron technology—a significant gap behind the most advanced Western technology (0.18 microns) at that time. China's most important limitations on progress at present are its inability to manufacture advanced lithography tools used in IC production, as well as a weak intellectual property infrastructure to encourage domestic innovation.[42]

---

[40] Cliff (2001), p. ix.

[41] This section summarizes the findings of Cliff (2001). In addition to microelectronics, computers, aviation, and space, this report provides detailed reviews of China's telecommunications, nuclear power, biotechnology, and chemical industries.

[42] Cliff (2001), pp. 11–14.

- Although China has become a major assembler of low-end personal computers—on a par with advanced industrial powers—its PCs are primarily composed of imported parts. One of China's major emerging strengths is an enormous pool of software professionals—by 1993 larger than any country in the world except the United States. China's progress in developing commercial software is still slow, however, again in no small measure due to the lack of protections against piracy.[43]
- China's aviation industry, after decades of relying on 1950s-era Soviet systems, has recently begun making much faster progress in aviation technology, owing in large part to cleverly crafted component coproduction agreements with major Western aircraft manufacturers.[44]
- China's space industry achieved a technological and political breakthrough in 2003 by successfully launching its first "taikonaut"—Lt. Col. Yang Liwei—into orbit and returning him safely to earth. Even before the manned launch, China's space industry had made significant progress—displaying impressive launch capacities, albeit with a somewhat high failure rate. Its satellite capacities, though limited, also included communications, photo reconnaissance, navigation, meteorological, remote sensing, and experimental satellites. The worldwide publicity Col. Yang's flight brought to China's technological progress will certainly strengthen the space program's claim on budgetary resources.[45]

China's overall technological capacities, as well as its specifically military technology, will still lag significantly behind the levels of the United States and Japan through the entire period that it crafts its responses to U.S. military transformation. While the PLA is presently

---

[43] Cliff (2001), pp. 14–16.

[44] Cliff (2001), pp. 24–27.

[45] Cliff (2001), pp. 27–30. See also John Baker and Kevin J. Pollpeter, "Red Dragon on the Rise? Strategic Implications of the Chinese Human Space Flight Program," *Space News*, December 19, 2004.

devoting considerable attention to ways of making more effective use of the commercial technology sector, this borrowing is still in an early stage, remains highly uneven across sectors, and has a strong ad hoc quality about it. Given this continuing technological gap, the financial resource pressures outlined above, and China's compelling concern about its military-technological gap with the United States, Beijing is most likely to turn to its most cheaply and easily available "off the shelf" technology packages in crafting its responses to U.S. military transformation. These responses will therefore most likely be built on a technological base not greatly beyond what China possesses today.

The Impact of Contextual Forces on China's Response Strategies

We anticipate that Beijing's responses to U.S. military transformation will exhibit many or most of the following general characteristics:

*   So long as regime survival and political instability remain Beijing's major security concerns, the overall structure of military modernization will be heavily influenced by the needs of stability. For example, because of their potential social control functions, PLA ground forces, and especially the paramilitary PAP, will continue to lay a more powerful claim on resources than would be justified solely by the needs of responding to U.S. military transformation. At present and for the foreseeable future, China faces no significant or immediate land border threat, and naval and air forces would be more critical to several possible strategies. Nevertheless, Beijing will continue to face major dilemmas in its efforts to free up resources through demobilization of PLA ground force units—including the problems of persuading local governments to arrange new homes and desirable jobs for these troops, and Beijing's related fear of the specter of large pools of unemployed or underemployed ex-servicemen and former defense factory workers.

- Also for reasons of stability, Beijing will probably favor responses that would, as a side benefit, avoid exacerbating its massive unemployment problem. This might involve favoring state-owned defense enterprises to keep their product lines running and avoid layoffs. Certainly, defense factories facing possible closure will invoke the specter of unrest in lobbying for their place in defense modernization plans. Fear of unrest could also introduce regional biases into Beijing's response to U.S. military transformation, as the leadership attempts to pump capital into highly unstable regions such as the northeast or the west.

- Within Beijing's halls of power, the growing budgetary competition for funds will almost certainly give a powerful political advantage to projects and responses that claim lower expenditures or can be accomplished with existing resources, and is likely to disadvantage projects with greater start-up costs, less certain prospects, or greater technological hurdles. Similarly, technologies sectors in which China's military and civilian commercial sectors have already shown greatest success will be easier to sell to the leadership.

- High prestige projects, such as the recently successful manned space program, will also enjoy a political advantage because of their perceived contribution to China's overall international image as a modern scientific-military power and the leadership's desire to appeal to Chinese nationalism. There is already evidence that other programs will attempt to secure their funding by "piggybacking" on the space program and other such politically popular programs.

- Although China has shown significant improvements in joint operations and has strengthened ties across bureaucratic and military service boundaries, these obstacles to organizational cooperation remain a powerful contextual factor. All things being equal, responses to U.S. military transformation that require less interservice, interagency, and civilian-military cooperation would be easier to adopt, and easier and cheaper to implement.

China will have little choice but to continue importing expensive weapon systems, particularly if Chinese leaders' perceptions of their international security environment compel them to raise armaments levels quickly. If budgetary pressures continue to expand, however, these programs are also likely to encounter rising competition, opposition, or delays. All of these problems would be greatly complicated by any cooling in China's relations with its most important weapons and technology supplier—Russia—with whom relations at present are unusually good by historical standards.

CHAPTER THREE

Chinese Counter-Transformation Options: A Methodological Introduction

Defining Network-Centric Warfare

To start, network-centric warfare rose up in contrast to platform-centric warfare, a tendency to design all equipment and operations around warfighting platforms: ships, aircraft, armor, and mobile guns. Every time a new capability was mooted it was evaluated by how it would enhance the warfighting power of the individual platform. Platforms were the pieces that were brought into battle; by counting who brought how many of which, one could calculate the correlation of forces, and get a sense of who would win.

NCW shifts the focus from the individual platform to the overall network, or more specifically, to the information resident on devices connected via the network. One aim is to create a total body of battlefield knowledge, not least of which is the precision location of enemy assets, that every component of warfare draws on or gives to. There are also other assets—processing capability, contacts to others on the network, even, potentially, weapons—that the network makes accessible regardless of where they are. In a network-centric world, every asset is judged, not on how well it enhances the platforms it sits on, but on how well it enhances the information and capabilities that are globally available. The difference, sometimes subtle and sometimes not, is between evaluating a new targeting pod on whether it makes an F-15 more effective or whether it provides information that, in networked conjunction with others sensors, tells warfighters where the enemy is. Because the latter could encompass all assets in a military, the level of integration is higher (but not necessarily harder) than for platform-centric warfare.

A considerable part of what makes NCW new, and more effective is in how militaries handle information. The conventional use of information followed the separation of intelligence and operations. Intelligence was generated from information collected on the enemy as to its intentions, assets, and locations. This created a generalized assessment of the adversary, which, in turn, permitted operations to be planned. But once these operations were planned, the basic warfighting units of the military—ships, squadrons, companies, etc.—used their own capabilities to prosecute the war. This is not to say the role of intelligence ended there; commanders still needed a flow of information to direct the allocation of assets. But the assets, once directed, fought with the information they largely gathered themselves.

By contrast, NCW entails collecting several orders of magnitude more data on the enemy (and on the environment in which the enemy could be operating). This information provides intelligence, but it also gives far more detailed guidance to the planning of specific operations. At best, an often-attained goal, it is possible to convert this information into specific targets that can then be prosecuted by a variety of weapons (in a sense, all network-accessible by the commander or controller). This process can take place within minutes, literally (e.g., if prosecuting fleeting or mobile targets). After the operation ends, battle damage assessment can be used to refine or re-apply the approach—again, within minutes. Here, real-time or near-real-time information becomes integral to conducting operations.

It is the relationship between NCW on the one hand and the exigencies of command and control on the other where room for differentiation lies. NCW can be fielded as variously concentrated or distributed. The former centralizes the collection of information and the making of decisions. For instance, information is collected from a limited number of highly capable sensors and trusted agents, is controlled and integrated in one place, and is parceled out to warfighters based on their need to know (i.e., what operations such information is meant to support). The match between targets and weapons, for instance, may be made at the top; the job of warfighters is to get the weapons close enough to the target to be effective. Nevertheless, what remains are the usual attributes of top-down command and control: the requirement for vertical coordination, the exercise of positive control, and the risks that centralization may lead to inflexibility in the face of ills ranging from effective network attack to individual dysfunctionality at the top.

A distributed form of NCW would rely on collecting information from a wide population of sensors and people (many of whom may be third parties). The information is made more broadly available, even on demand, in some cases and is fused in multiple, often competing, centers. Warfighters, with access to semi-processed and finished intelligence (and with some ability to "task" the system) are given broad mission orders and sufficient discretion to meet commanders' objectives. One sees the usual attributes of empowered delegation: peer-to-peer coordination, the exercise of negative control, and the risks that decentralization may lead to emergent faults as uncoordinated plans each hamper the execution of one another.

There are some distinct advantages of being able to implement a distributed form of NCW. Forces can be dispersed, which makes it harder for adversaries (especially those armed with chemical or nuclear weapons) to target them. They can also be lighter and faster, but at the same time more lethal. Yet, such advantages are less the result of NCW per se and more the result of having over-the-horizon (OTH) firepower on call. Once warfighters are freed from having to carry anything but light ammunition, they are naturally more mobile and less tied to their stockpiles. Where NCW comes in is in the ability of dispersed warfighters to detect, geolocate, and call back for fires on enemies.

As a first-order approximation, the United States favors, at least rhetorically, the distributed approach. China's PLA, as best we can guess, is more likely to evolve toward the concentrated approach. Yet both approaches are ideal types, and the correlation to national styles of warfare is only approximate. Neither is ipso facto better than the other. A good deal depends on the nature of the conflict they are suited for: the circumstances (e.g., conventional conflict vs. irregular operations; predominantly land vs. predominantly sea), the enemy (e.g., its sophistication and warfighting style), and the assets one has for the occasion. The cultural issues noted earlier are themselves not trivial ones; militaries are necessarily a reflection of their society and always will be. Perhaps most important is not the approach but the capacity for flexibility: As a rule, it would be wiser to adjust the concentrated or distributed mix to the war than to understand the war in light of the mix.

Typologizing Chinese Response Options

This report examines four notional Chinese response options to U.S. military transformation. Each is used as a heuristic to tease out potentially threatening developments for U.S. forces. While they are discussed in isolation, developments in China suggest that all or portions of each strategy are being pursued in earnest, and some combination of the options will likely characterize the final configuration.

Option One is labeled "conventional modernization 'plus'." It examines only operations using a modified version of conventional weapons and strategies. It does not address Chinese ground-to-ground missile operations (see Option Three) or air attacks against U.S. ground bases, but does discuss Chinese writings on space warfare. The primary foci of the chapter are operations against naval targets and space assets. These high-tech operations may facilitate a traditional amphibious or even triphibious invasion of Taiwan. However, because an amphibious operation does not appear to be countertransformational and would, in fact, appear to be especially vulnerable to U.S. transformation efforts, the over-water assault is not explored in detail.

Option Two outlines the wide range of oft-cited nontraditional coercion operations that China could use against Taiwan and the United States, including fifth-column sabotage and the use of Spetnaz-like special forces on the island, and information operations ranging from psychological operations to CNA. The analysis is built around two perceived Chinese centers of gravity in a Taiwan scenario: the will of the Taiwanese people and U.S. military intervention. Particular emphasis is placed on Chinese perceptions and misperceptions of the balance of forces in these two dimensions, and assessments of the potential success of U.S. countermoves is offered.

Option Three is a "missile-centric" strategy, designed to present an overwhelming short-range missile threat to Taiwan, improve China's offensive capabilities against U.S. bases in the Asia-Pacific, and give the PLA the capability to launch conventional strikes against U.S. strategic targets. Chapter Six initially examines the utility of nuclear weapons to counter U.S. military transformation, but argues that China's lack of counterforce capabilities limits their usefulness as counter-transformational weapons. On the conventional side, the analysis considers not only further improvements in China's short-range ballistic missile (SRBM) arsenal, but also several more speculative possibilities, such as future developments in strategy and force structure that might give China the capability to wage theater and strategic conventional warfare against U.S. targets in Guam, Hawaii, and the continental United States (CONUS) with conventionally armed ballistic and cruise missiles. These "high-end" capabilities would be focused against a small set of high-leverage targets that would influence both the political and military underpinnings of operations against China, consistent with relatively modest numbers of delivery systems.

Option Four outlines the parameters of possible Chinese NCW warfare strategies, with particular emphasis on the unique NCW strategies that could emerge from China's unique technological, cultural, and organizational contexts. A concluding appendix offers two possible U.S. counterresponses to the development of a Chinese network-centric military. The first, labeled "enhancing NCW," follows the current trajectory of NCW on its logical course to distributed sensors and unmanned platforms, while the second counter, described as "transcending NCW," explores the use of biometrics in a world of ubiquitous sensors and shooters.

CHAPTER FOUR
Option One: Conventional Modernization "Plus"

China's military strategy has gone through an evolution since the PLA was founded in 1927. While People's War still remains an important tenet in PLA warfighting, it has been supplanted by other strategies more suitable to waging war with high-technology weapons. As a result, China's military strategy is no longer focused on luring an enemy in deep to overwhelm it with mass human wave attacks. Rather, the ability of modern militaries to conduct highly mobile operations and long-range precision strikes coupled with the recognition that China must meet the enemy away from its border to protect its vital economic and political centers has led the PLA to focus on developing area and access denial strategies and the technology to implement them.

This chapter examines the Chinese descriptions of armed conflict, the principles it plans to use to fight these conflicts, and the implications for U.S. military transformation. The chapter concludes that the PLA does not wish to fight the U.S. military force-on-force; rather, it is studying ways in which it can conduct attacks against key nodes that would paralyze an enemy or open up opportunities to conduct decisive attacks. As the U.S. military becomes more information intensive, these types of attacks present critical implications for U.S. transformation efforts.

From People's War to Local War Under High-Tech Conditions

The Chinese taxonomy of armed conflict is divided into three levels: war, campaigns, and battles. Wars are composed of several decisive campaigns that are strategic in nature and directly connected with the country's political, economic, and diplomatic policies. Campaigns, on the other hand, are limited in geographic scope but still serve the nation's political, economic, and diplomatic requirements. Battles are tactical operations that serve the goals of campaigns.[1]

Based on the study of conflicts since the early 1980s, especially Operation Desert Storm, PLA theorists have judged that the next conflict China fights will not be a total war but will most likely be a limited war of short duration and limited in geographic scope and objectives. Furthermore, the next conflict will involve the intense use of high technology. High technology will manifest itself in improved reconnaissance abilities, over the horizon precision weapons, and high-speed mobility that will enable both sides to rapidly process intelligence, achieve local superiority, and conduct precision strikes against the enemy's vital targets. The Chinese conceptualization of this type of modern war centers on the term *local war under high-tech conditions.*[2]

Because modern wars will occupy a smaller geographic region and its actors will pursue limited objectives, and the fact that modern militaries are more mobile and able to deliver large amounts of precision munitions in a short period of time, high-tech local wars will be shorter in duration than total war and may involve only one or two campaigns. The implication of this for the PLA is that because victory will be decided in relatively short order, the PLA's actions prior to

---

[1] He Dingqing, *A Course on the Science of Campaigns* (战役学教程), Beijing: Military Science Press, 2001, p. 239.

[2] He (2001), pp. 239–240.

and at the outset of armed conflict will be critical.[3] In the words of one Chinese analyst: "In a limited high-tech war, where the pace of action is fast and the duration short, a campaign often takes on a make-or-break character. Clearly the quick and decisive battle assumes much more importance in such a war."[4]

PLA Strategic Response to High-Tech Enemies

This characterization of future war raises a dilemma for the PLA. PLA writers acknowledge that it would be difficult for the PLA to prevail against a high-tech opponent like the U.S. military. Indeed, Chinese analysts bluntly acknowledge that China's military technology is inferior to the U.S. military and that this situation will not change for the foreseeable future.[5] As a passage in Wang and Zhang's *Science of Campaigns* explains:

> The most salient objective reality that the PLA will face in future campaign operations is the fact that it will be using inferior weapons to deal with an enemy that has superior arms.[6]

The relative technological inferiority of the PLA has led Chinese strategists to develop a way in which the "inferior can defeat the superior" (以劣胜优). While the United States is regarded as having the most powerful military, PLA theorists contend that the U.S. military cannot be strong in every aspect. According one writer, "If China confronts an enemy with high technology and superior equipment in

---

[3] Nan Li, "The PLA's Evolving Campaign Doctrine and Strategies," in James C. Mulvenon and Richard H. Yang, eds., *The People's Liberation Army in the Information Age*, Santa Monica, Calif.: RAND Corporation, CF-145-CAPP/AF, 1999, pp. 149–150.

[4] Lu Linzhi, "Preemptive Strikes Are Crucial in Limited High-Tech Wars," *Jiefangjun bao*, February 7, 1996.

[5] See, for example, Peng Guangqian and Yao Youzhi, eds., *The Science of Strategy* (战略学), Beijing: Military Science Press, 2001, pp. 466–467.

[6] See Wang Houqing (王厚卿) and Zhang Xingye (张兴业), eds., *Science of Campaigns* (战役学), Beijing: National Defense University Press, 2000 (esp. Chapter 3 on the "Objective Conditions of PLA").

a local war, it is impossible that the enemy would also have comprehensive superiority in politics, diplomacy, geography, and support."[7] Thus, one way of compensating for China's weakness is to devise strategies that will maximize China's relative strengths and create opportunities to exploit the United States' weaknesses.[8] This is reiterated in numerous sources, including an internal volume on the study of campaigns, which states, "only by using its areas of strength to strike at the enemy's weakness can the PLA achieve campaign victory in future wars against aggression."[9]

A comprehensive review of Chinese military writings reveals several themes on meeting the challenges of fighting the U.S. military. These themes are broadly covered under two principles: seizing the initiative and attacking an adversary's center of gravity.

Seizing the Initiative

One overriding theme in Chinese military writings is seizing the initiative. Because high-tech local wars are decided rapidly, victory usually goes to the military that is able to seize the initiative at the outset of the campaign. As one source argues: "the initiative is a military operation's freedom. If initiative is lost, then a military will be destroyed and will lose."[10] Waiting for a high-tech adversary to fully deploy its forces before attacking is to invite failure, especially for weaker militaries. One oft-mentioned example is Iraq's failure to attack coalition forces prior to the start of Operation Desert Storm when coalition forces were still in the deployment phase.[11] In the

---

[7] Jiang Lei (蔣磊), *Modern Strategy for Using the Inferior to Defeat the Superior* (现代以劣胜优战略), Beijing: National Defense University Press, 1997, pp. 113–114.

[8] For one example among the many sources that address this topic, see Jiang (1997), pp. 35–41. Jiang discusses the PLA's history of fighting against enemies with superior equipment and technology in the Chinese civil war, the war against Japan, and the Korean War. In addition, Jiang notes that it was Mao Zedong who, at a meeting in September 1953, first officially raised the formulation of "using inferior equipment to defeat an enemy with superior equipment" (以劣势装备战胜优势装备之敌).

[9] Wang and Zhang (2000), p. 25.

[10] He (2001), p. 150.

[11] Lu Linzhi (1996).

words of one Chinese analyst, "If [the PLA] just sits there and waits for the enemy to complete assembling its full array of troops, China's fighting potential will certainly be more severely jeopardized because the enemy will then be in a position to put its overall combat superiority to good use, making it more difficult for China to win the war."[12] Moreover, "For the weaker party, waiting for the enemy to deliver the first blow will have disastrous consequences and may even put it in a passive situation from which it will never be able to get out."[13]

Seizing the initiative is a core element of the PLA's overall strategic concept of "active defense." Active defense stresses striking only after being struck first and basing oneself on home territory. The operational guidance provided by active defense, however, is to stress active operations to seize the initiative.[14] Consequently, active defense can be thought of as strategically defensive but operationally offensive.

One frequently mentioned method of seizing the initiative is to "gain mastery by striking first." PLA officers are taught to have a very strong "offensive mentality."[15] The PLA must continually go on the offensive to seize the initiative or to exploit successes in combat. Two important aspects of gaining mastery by striking first are surprise attacks and preemptive strikes.

Surprise. Chinese strategists recognize that attaining some degree of surprise may be necessary to effectively seize the initiative in a conflict with an adversary as powerful as the United States. Indeed, numerous Chinese strategists emphasize achieving victory through surprise (出奇制胜), by striking at an unexpected time and in an unanticipated place.[16] In one recent internal volume, Chinese mili-

---

[12] Lu Linzhi (1996).

[13] Lu Linzhi (1996).

[14] Wang and Zhang (2000), p. 90.

[15] He (2001), p. 148.

[16] See, for instance, Peng and Yao (2001), p. 307.

tary writers highlight the importance of surprise, defining it and describing its potential results as follows:

> Taking the enemy by surprise would catch it unprepared and cause confusion in and huge psychological pressure on the enemy, and would help one win relatively large victories at relatively small costs.[17]

Once surprise is achieved, the PLA must exploit it decisively as quickly as possible:

> Under modern conditions, it is difficult to sustain surprise, which can only exist at the initial period of time. Therefore, once surprise is achieved, one must move quickly to exploit and expand the initial battle success, so as not to let the enemy regain its footing from the confusion.[18]

The problem remains, however, as to how China will be able to conduct such operations in the face of the clear superiority the U.S. military holds over Chinese forces, especially in ISR. Chinese analysts express their concerns that surprise is becoming more difficult to achieve, though they assess that it is still possible:

> To well disguise one's own intent is an important element in taking the enemy by surprise. The objective of disguising one's intent can be achieved through camouflage, deception, feint, and under bad weather. Although it has become more difficult to disguise one's intent under modern conditions, modern campaign practice has proved that it is still possible to take the enemy by surprise through excellent stratagem, smart camouflage, deception, feint, and under bad weather conditions. With the development in disguising technology and equipment, it is particularly important to deceive and mislead the enemy by high

---

[17] Wang and Zhang (2000), pp. 108–110.

[18] Wang and Zhang (2000), pp. 108–110.

tech means so as to truly hide one's intent and achieve victory by taking the enemy by surprise.[19]

In terms of timing, it is critical to strike before the superior adversary has a chance to initiate its own attack or when it is still deploying its forces and building up its strength. According to one Chinese writer, "The enemy is most vulnerable during the early phase of the war when it is still deploying troops and making operational preparations."[20] Similarly, the authors of a Chinese book on U.S. military strategy view the deployment phase as a critical period of weakness for the United States:

> In the opening stage, it is impossible to rapidly transfer enormous forces to the battlefield. Thus [the United States] is unable to establish superiority of forces and firepower, and it is easy for the U.S. military to be forced into a passive position from the start; this could very possibly have an impact on the process and outcome of the conflict.[21]

To this end, one possibility mentioned in an internal volume is using a military exercise as cover for the preparations that would precede an attack.[22]

A number of Chinese authors write about the usefulness of preemptive strikes, especially for weaker militaries. According to PLA authors, defeat for a weaker force will already be determined once a more powerful military is fully deployed. Consequently, conducting a preemptive strike may be the most effective solution for a weaker force to seize the initiative early in the campaign. A quick strike prior to or quickly following the formal declaration of hostilities would disrupt U.S. deployment of forces to the region, place the United States

---

[19] Wang and Zhang (2000), pp. 108–110.

[20] Lu Linzhi (1996).

[21] Pan Xiangting (潘湘庭) and Zhanping Sun (孙占平), eds., *The U.S. Military in Local Wars Under High-Tech Conditions* (高技术条件下美军局部战争), Beijing: PLA Press, 1994, p. 238.

[22] Wang and Zhang (2000), p. 330.

in a passive position, and deliver a psychological shock to the United States and its allies. As one Chinese source argues:

> This makes it imperative that China launches a preemptive strike by taking advantage of the window of opportunity present before the enemy acquires a high tech edge or develops a full-fledged combat capability in the war zone. Through a preemptive strike, China can put good timing and geographical location and the support of the people to good use by making a series of offensive moves to destroy the enemy's ability to deploy high-tech weapons and troops and limit its ability to acquire a high-tech edge in the war zone, thus weakening its capacity to mount a powerful offensive. This is the only way to steer the course of the war in a direction favorable to China.[23]

Accordingly, one Chinese analyst writes:

> [A]n effective strategy by which the weaker party can overcome its more powerful enemy is to take advantage of serious gaps in the deployment of forces by the enemy with a high-tech edge by launching a preemptive strike during the early phase of the war or in the preparations leading to the offensive.[24]

In the words of another Chinese analyst:

> This lengthy period of war preparations undoubtedly provides an adversary with quite a few opportunities that it can exploit, by launching a surprise attack or cutting off supply lines, for instance, causing the enemy to collapse without a battle because it is unable to receive supplies in a timely fashion.[25]

Preemptive action appears to conflict with the PLA's guideline of "striking only after the enemy has struck" (后发制人). Preemptive

---

[23] Lu Linzhi (1996).

[24] Lu Linzhi (1996).

[25] Li Qingshan (李庆山), *The RMA and High-Tech War* (新军事革命与高技术战争), Beijing: Military Sciences Press, 1995.

strikes, however, are viewed as consistent with China's "active defense" strategy, as suggested by the following passage:

> The so-called preemptive strike means taking a series of decisive offensive actions in a battle to attack key targets of the enemy's in-depth campaign formations, diminishing its high-tech edge, impairing its readiness to attack, and creating an advantageous combat situation, all within a strategic framework of gaining mastery by striking only after the enemy has struck.[26]

This paradox is explained by defining an enemy's first strike as any action that indicates preparation for military action. Thus, any U.S. military support or deployment that is deemed to be a precursor to U.S. action could be grounds for a preemptive strike.[27] This type of rationalization thus gives China a moral fig leaf to not appear as an aggressor, as demonstrated during the "self-defense counterattack" against Vietnam in 1979.

Attacking the Center of Gravity (破机重心)

While the attention given to "gaining mastery by striking first" provides insights into the offensive character of Chinese strategy, the discussion of attacking an adversary's center of gravity illustrates the types of targets that may be the focus of attack. Attacking the center of gravity is described as

> attacking an enemy's political, military, economic and social systems, especially those directly related to operations, to destroy or damage primary targets in order to dismember or paralyze the whole system so as to destroy its operational determination and accomplish the goals necessary for victory.[28]

---

[26] Li Qingshan (1995). The final part of the previous sentence conveys China's view that a preemptive attack is not a first strike. This is the case because it follows certain actions by the enemy, perhaps including declaration of its intent to intervene and/or deployment of forces to the theater, which China would see as equivalent to the initiation of a conflict.

[27] Li Qingshan (1995).

[28] He (2001), p. 244.

Unlike in the past, attacking the enemy's center of gravity no longer focuses on attacking the enemy's forces. Rather, the focus is now on attacking critical targets such as command nodes and logistics and information systems. Under this type of strategy, the PLA would initially not try to conduct a wholesale destruction of enemy forces but would instead determine a target or target set so critical that its destruction would gravely affect operations and bring about victory. Attacking an enemy's center of gravity has advantages over other types of strategies. First, a military can more easily seize the initiative by attacking the center of gravity. Second, because attacking the center of gravity can paralyze a whole military, it can accomplish the goal of a "quick war to achieve a quick resolution" (速战速决). Third, attacking the center of gravity is the best way to achieve largest effect.[29]

Key Point Strikes (重点打击). Attacking an enemy's center of gravity is closely related to the PLA's guiding concept of "key point strikes." Key point strikes are described as

> the concentration of forces in the main direction of the military campaign, at the critical juncture, and for a major operation, with an objective of mounting focused strikes against targets vital to sustaining and supporting the enemy's operational system. Destroying and annihilating such vital targets and quickly paralyzing the enemy's operational system should become the focus of campaign execution and the main approach to achieving campaign victory.... In directing a campaign, the key to carrying out the concept of key point strikes is to correctly determine the vital targets for key point strikes while at the same time concentrating the necessary force to strike at those vital targets. Both are indispensable.[30]

Or as one passage puts it, key point attacks are intended to "paralyze first and annihilate later."[31]

---

[29] He (2001), pp. 244–245.

[30] Wang and Zhang (2000), p. 96 [authors' translation].

[31] Wang and Zhang (2000), p. 89.

"Key points" are defined as targets

that could have a direct impact on the overall situation of the campaign or produce an overall effect. They include systems, parts, and links vital to the sustaining of the campaign, as well as important force groupings and important battlefield facilities.[32]

To successfully launch key point strikes against the enemy's centers of gravity, it is first necessary to identify those key points. *Science of Campaigns* states that key points may differ according to adversary, but in the case of a strong high-tech adversary,

one should select the enemy's information systems, command systems, and support systems as targets for key point strikes. As for ordinary combat adversaries, one should determine targets for key point strike based on the objective of annihilating the enemy's effective force strength.[33]

Science of Campaigns lists five types of targets that, if sufficiently degraded or destroyed, could tip the balance in favor of the PLA. Those targets are command systems (指挥系统), information systems (信息系统), weapon systems (武器系统), logistics systems (后勤系统), and, finally, the linkages between these various systems. While this source does not explicitly prioritize this list, the fact that command systems and information systems are the first two target types mentioned suggests that these may be the two most important target types. Placing these two target types at the top of the list would be similar to U.S. strategy and consistent with the numerous Chinese writings on the importance of achieving information superiority.

Achieve Information Superiority. Many Chinese writers regard information collection, processing, and transmission and the denial of those capabilities to an adversary as vital to the successful prosecution of a modern high-tech warfare. Peng and Yao's *Science of Strategy* states:

---

[32] Wang and Zhang (2000), p. 96.
[33] Wang and Zhang (2000), p. 97.

> Information supremacy is the precondition for achieving
> supremacy in the air, at sea, and on the ground and is critical to
> achieving and maintaining battlefield supremacy. Information
> operations are unavoidably the most important operational
> method of modern wars.[34]

According to many Chinese writings, information supremacy is the precondition for achieving supremacy in the air, at sea, and on the ground and is critical to achieving and maintaining battlefield supremacy. Consequently, information operations are unavoidably the most important operational method of modern wars.[35]

As a result of the growing significance of information in conducting high-tech war, "information warfare" has become an increasingly important subject among PLA strategists. *Science of Campaigns* describes information warfare as

> a means, not a goal. The goal of information warfare is, at the
> critical time and region related to overall campaign operations,
> to cut off the enemy's ability to obtain, control, and use information, to influence, reduce, and even destroy the enemy's
> capabilities of observing, decision-making, and commanding
> and controlling troops, while we maintain our own ability to
> command and control in order to seize information superiority,
> and to produce the strategic and campaign superiority, creating
> conditions for winning the decisive battle.[36]

One author asserts

> the operational objectives of the two sides on attack and defense
> are neither the seizing of territory nor the killing of so many
> enemies, but rather the paralyzing of the other side's information system and the destruction of the other side's will to resist.
> The enemy's command centers, communication hubs, information processing centers, high-tech weapon control systems, and
> supply systems could become priority targets of attack. The

---

[34] Peng and Yao (2001), p. 358.

[35] Peng and Yao (2001), p. 358 [authors' translation].

[36] Wang and Zhang (2000), p. 169 [authors' translation].

scenes in the past of close-combat fighting have become history, and where the front and the rear are located is no longer an issue of concern to commanders and units.[37]

The conduct of information warfare also places great emphasis on the concept of "gaining mastery by striking first." In fact, conducting information operations not only facilitates but may actually require striking first. Specifically, information operations rely

> more on taking early advantage to seize control over information. This is decided by the characteristics of information warfare. First of all, an information offensive is mainly launched by remote combat and covert method, making it easier to launch a sudden attack. Secondly, information warfare consumes fewer human resource and material resources than the conventional combat of forces, so it has stronger sustainability. Once the offensive starts, it can go on incessantly for a long time. Thirdly, information systems operate in the electromagnetic spectrum. Therefore, any operating information system on the battlefield is exposed. Theoretically speaking, it is impossible for an operating information system to completely protect itself from enemy's information offensive. Moreover, physical destruction during an information offensive also makes it difficult for the defender to restore the system in a short period of time. These characteristics of information warfare show that whoever takes the early advantage is more likely to seize control over information on the battlefield, and achieve a better combat effect. In this sense, active offense requires that in information warfare on the battlefield, we should not only use the offense as our main means, but we should also "gain mastery by striking first."[38]

Key point attacks are also stressed in information warfare. Of the four important types of campaign operations discussed in *Science of Campaigns* (information warfare, combined firepower operations, mobility, and special warfare), attacks against key points are men-

---

[37] Chen Huan, "The Third Military Revolution," in Michael Pillsbury, ed., *Chinese Views of Future Warfare*, Washington, D.C.: National Defense University Press, 1998, p. 393.

[38] Wang and Zhang, 2000, p. 178.

tioned only in the information warfare section. In fact, *Science of Campaigns* specifically refers to concentrating "the forces of an information offensive at the very beginning of a campaign to directly attack the vital parts and key links of enemy information systems, destroying enemy information systems first and paralyzing the whole enemy combat system to get the largest victory with least cost."[39]

Information superiority, however, does not need to be continually held. According to one source, information superiority may only need to be achieved during critical periods of a campaign:

> For any strong army, establishing information control is a relative concept and absolute information control does not exist. For our army it is even more so. The process of establishing information control is relative with the scope of control being localized and the gains and losses dynamic. The most important value of information operations is when they are needed by joint operations, the scope of seizure is relative like this with localized information control increasing effectiveness.[40]

While information warfare attacks can assume a variety of forms, they generally fall into two main categories: "soft-kill" methods and "hard-kill" methods. "Soft-kill" methods include CNA and electronic jamming. Some can be carried out clandestinely, are deniable, and their effects are often temporary. "Hard-kill" methods, on the other hand, cause physical destruction and can be carried out through the use of ballistic and cruise missiles, special operations forces, air strikes, microwave weapons, lasers, particle beam weapons, and nuclear and nonnuclear electromagnetic pulse (EMP) weapons. The physical destruction caused by hard kills is described as the only method that can thoroughly paralyze information systems and infrastructure.[41] The targets of these weapons include command personnel, command and control facilities, communication centers, com-

---

[39] Wang and Zhang, 2000, p. 179.

[40] Dai Qingmin (戴清民), ed., *Introduction to Information Operations* (信息作战概论), Beijing: PLA Press, 1999, pp. 276–277.

[41] Dai (1999), p. 272.

puter systems, command and control aircraft, and communication satellites.

Assessment of Chinese Strategy

Chinese strategy focuses on avoiding direct confrontation with the U.S. military and instead emphasizes attacking U.S. vulnerabilities that can lead to decisively seizing the initiative. Following this strategy, the PLA could be expected to select certain systems or platforms for concentrated attack. This type of strategy places more importance on air, missile, and naval assets rather than ground assets, whose ability to strike U.S. information systems, for example, is negligible, with the possible extreme exception of special forces units.[42] In the event of an invasion of Taiwan, this strategy calls for high-tech measures to pave the way for a traditional amphibious operation. Consequently, because an amphibious operation does not appear to be counter-transformational and would, in fact, appear to be especially vulnerable to U.S. transformation efforts, the next section of this chapter involves only those strategies and technologies that are counter-transformational and thus not ground forces.

Operationalizing Chinese Strategies with Conventional Forces

China's use of conventional forces to attack the U.S. military holds several advantages. First, the PLA already has a large conventional force that could be immediately used in a conflict. Its possession of a small number of advanced platforms, such as Su-27s and *Kilo*-class submarines, could be used to exploit the vulnerabilities described above while many of its less advanced or outdated platforms could be used in mass follow on attacks to exploit successes. Second, the technology used, in many cases, may be familiar and doctrine concerning their use may have already been developed and training may have

---

[42] This exception would most likely have to involve the insertion of commandos to attack U.S. bases or infrastructure.

already been conducted. Third, in the case of a conflict over Taiwan or some other contingency on its border, the basing of its forces on home territory eliminates the need for reliance on allies. It also allows the PLA to establish a defense in depth and dispersal of forces over a wide area. Geography thus may limit the effectiveness of air strikes as U.S. aircraft could be expected to remain in hostile air space to attack widely dispersed targets.

China clearly needs to meld key point strikes with conventional operations, yet it still lacks the types of equipment or the numbers required to fight a full-scale high-tech war against the United States. Despite this, the PLA does write about using conventional forces in a manner that is consistent with the strategy of attacking key points. PLA conventional operations can affect U.S. transformation efforts in two ways. The first is through operations against U.S. naval assets, particularly against aircraft carrier battle groups (CVBGs), with the goal of damaging, sinking, or forcing these assets to operate at distances beyond optimal operating range. The second is through attacks on U.S. space assets with the goal of degrading or destroying critical communication links, denying intelligence to U.S. commanders, or depriving U.S. forces the use of Global Positioning System (GPS)–guided munitions or navigation.

Attacks Against Naval Targets

In discussing the need to attack naval targets, PLA writings are forthright about the challenges of countering a navy with advanced weaponry. One source enumerates the deficiencies of the People's Liberation Army Navy (PLAN) as follows:

> The most prominent problem is the difficulty in concentrating force to create superiority. This is because: 1) The technology level of the main equipment of our navy is relatively backward and its capability is deficient, especially its reconnaissance and warning capability, command and control, and electronic warfare countermeasures. Therefore they are at disadvantage when compared to comparable opposing ships. 2) Our navy's force is light and mainly consists of medium and small ships. Therefore, individual operational capability is weak. 3) In order to defend

against an enemy attack, the navy's campaign forces are dispersed, making it difficult to form a strong operational capability in the operational area in a short period of time. Because of the reasons above, there will be many difficulties in destroying the enemy forces, concentrating force, and creating superiority.[43]

This same source goes on to list the advantages of an unnamed naval opponent:

In comparison to our opponent, [our navy's] ability to maneuver is weak, and its reconnaissance and early warning are deficient and is limited to the areas that it can control. Therefore, it is difficult to recognize enemy weaknesses and quickly conduct strike...

The enemy's medium and large ships often have aircraft or helicopters and medium range anti-ship and anti-air missiles. It has long-range reconnaissance and early warning capabilities and the area it can control is large. It can conduct long-range offensive and defensive operations. Therefore they ordinarily do not enter an enemy's littorals and especially do not lightly enter into the range of an enemy's missile.

The ocean areas near our country have many islands that can be used, but most of them are nearby and are of limited use for controlling an area. These islands can be conveniently used by our navy, but it will be difficult to surround an enemy force that is conducting long range operations. For our forces, especially submarines, to advance on the enemy and spend a long time in the operational radius of the enemy will present serious dangers...

Destroying the enemy naval force involves conducting an offensive campaign by, for example, amply preparing equipment, and selecting a beneficial operational time and area. Because our navy's technology and equipment is inferior, however, especially its electronic warfare capability, warning capability, and anti-air

---

[43] Chen Fangyou (陈访友), *Naval Campaign Teaching Materials* (海军战役学教程), Beijing: National Defense University Press, 1991.

capability, it will be difficult to achieve surprise when approaching the enemy. Moreover, it will be likely to encounter enemy defensive strikes and counter strikes. Under this type of situation, the offensive and defensive operations between us and the enemy will change frequently and superiority can change hands.[44]

Another difficulty to overcome is the vastness of the ocean and the scarcity of ships to patrol every avenue of approach. Chinese analysts recognize that China does not have the necessary resources to conduct such a campaign and recommends that the PLAN choose one or several directions and focus its resources on attacking those sea-lanes. Such a strategy could have disastrous consequences if the wrong sea-lanes were picked:

> The nature of targets for sea transportation sabotage campaign are various, and the targets are scattered in a wide area, they are in many places over a wide area, and combat time is continuous and long. Therefore, according to the goal of a sea transportation sabotage campaign, the importance of enemy transportation lines, and the conditions of the sea area, we should choose one direction or one to several transportation lines of enemy to focus sea transportation sabotage combat. So we have to deploy our forces judiciously.[45]

Another source states that this strategy is the only way "the contradiction of 'many lines and few troops' can be resolved and local superiority created to obtain a relatively good effect."[46]

But, in an apparent attempt to make the best out of a bad situation, this same source expounds on the virtues of having a small force that can only attack in one direction:

> Low intensity strikes use a relatively small amount of force and weapons to strike targets. They require fewer supplies to con-

---

[44] Chen Fangyou (1991), pp. 220–221 [authors' translation].

[45] Wang and Zhang (2000), pp. 325–326.

[46] Chen Fangyou (1991), p. 190.

tinuously deplete and weaken the enemy, dissipate the enemy's attention and bring chaos to the enemy's deployments by forcing him to concentrate his forces. Using a small force is convenient, coordination is simple, and it is easy to insure reliability. Therefore, it is easier to organize while presenting the enemy with a comprehensive threat. A small force can even be divided into ship forces and air forces and can also use submarines. Its area of operation is based on determined needs and capabilities.[47]

To overcome its deficiencies, the PLA may also try to wait for opportune times to conduct attacks against naval vessels. Chinese analysts state that naval vessels are particularly vulnerable when a naval group is being redeployed, is undergoing resupply, is passing through a narrow waterway, or when the weather is bad.[48]

Perhaps the most potent type of naval force is the CVBG. CVBGs not only pose significant problems for the PLAN, but they would also likely play a major role in U.S. efforts to maintain air superiority over Taiwan and to attack targets on the mainland. According to one Chinese writer, the United States sometimes relies on aircraft carriers for 80 percent of its air power.[49] Because of this, aircraft carriers are also described as "a great threat to anti-air operations in littoral areas and should be resolutely countered."[50]

Chinese analysts do not believe that aircraft carriers are invincible, however, and have identified weaknesses they think could be exploited:

- Because of its large size, a CVBG is difficult to conceal and is detectable by radar, infrared, and sonar. In addition, because of

---

[47] Chen Fangyou (1991), p. 191.

[48] Chen Fangyou (1991), p. 227.

[49] Wei Yuejiang (魏岳江), "Our Army Explores New Methods for Countering Enemy Over the Horizon Operations" (图文: 我军探究新战法抗强敌远程超视距作战), *Liberation Army Daily* (解放军报) (online), January 27, 2003.

[50] Cui Changqi (崔长崎), *21st Century Air Attacks and Counter Air Attacks* (二十一世纪空袭与反空袭), Beijing: PLA Press, 2002, p. 215.

its large size, an aircraft carrier is easier to hit than other types of vessels.

- Air operations from an aircraft carrier can be affected by weather.
- A CVBG consumes an immense amount of supplies.
- CVBGs have poor antisubmarine and antimine capabilities.
- The hulls and flight decks of aircraft carriers are susceptible to damage by armor-piercing munitions.
- While aircraft carriers do carry a large number of planes, the number of planes actually devoted to air defense is small, around 20. In addition, aircraft launching is sometimes restricted by maneuvers.[51] Thus, it would be possible to overwhelm an aircraft carrier's air defense during certain times.

Several tactics can be used to attack aircraft carriers with ballistic missiles, submarines, antiship missiles, and mines. An article in the Chinese journal *Naval and Merchant Ships* (舰船知识), describing Soviet submarine tactics, states that submarines should lie in wait for a CVBG and ambush it with antiship missiles. The first wave of the strike would use a combination of antiship missiles and anti-radiation missiles against ships providing protection to the aircraft to weaken the battle group's antimissile capability, but also states that going after the carrier in the first wave may be preferable.[52] Another source recommends first shooting down an aircraft carrier's early warning aircraft and states "only by first destroying command, detection, and guidance aircraft can the operational capability of an aircraft carrier

---

[51] Guo Xilin, "The Aircraft Carrier Formation Is Not an Unbreakable Barrier," *Guangming Ribao*, December 26, 2000. (Major General Guo is the director of the Air Force Radar Academy.)

[52] "The Oscar Class: Organizing and Implementing Anti-Ship Operations," *Jianchuan Zhishi*, December 1, 2002. See also, for example, Liu Jiangping, Zhu Weitao, and Hu Zili, "A Move Essential for Disintegrating the Enemy's Combined Aerial Attacks: If the Federal Republic of Yugoslavia Attacked NATO's Aircraft Carrier-Led Battle Groups in the Adriatic Sea," *Liberation Army Daily*, August 17, 1999.

be weakened."[53] This would also assist the execution of low-level air attacks on an aircraft carrier from several directions.[54]

Another source goes into great detail about a three-stage attack against naval ships using information warfare methods. The first stage is the force deployment stage, in which electronic monitoring by coastal-, sea-, air-, and space-based reconnaissance platforms would locate and collect information on the disposition, location, and direction of movement of an enemy naval force. The PLA would also use deception techniques to misdirect or disperse enemy reconnaissance platforms to make them less able to determine its real objective. This could involve using cover and concealment as well as fake radio and radar signals. Unmanned aerial vehicles (UAVs) and floating radar reflectors could be used to confuse the air battle space while fake submarines and periscopes flood the sea battle space. Finally, communications would be strictly controlled so as not to reveal the true direction or actual forces used.

The second stage is the weakening stage, in which the PLA would try to tire out and weaken the enemy in order to create the conditions for a concentrated attack. UAVs could harass enemy ships and cause the redeployment of enemy early warning and electronic warfare planes and reduce the sortie rate of enemy fighter planes. Small vessels and fishing boats could place radar reflectors into the water to simulate naval operations. Civilian vessels could also be used to place radar reflectors, fake submarines, and fake periscopes "to create a complex electromagnetic naval battlefield" to force the enemy to make mistakes.

The final stage is the sudden attack phase. During this phase, hard kills could be used to

> paralyze the enemy's electronic information systems. We can use the Second Artillery or the Air Force to deliver an EMP bomb to the enemy's large naval force to destroy the enemy's warning and detection systems and operational command systems and other

---

[53] Wei Yuejiang (2003).

[54] Guo (2000).

electronic information systems, and can use the air force to attack ship-borne radar and early warning aircraft radar with anti-radiation missiles to paralyze or partially paralyze the enemy's warning and detection systems and operational command systems.[55]

Soft-kill methods could be used to jam communication satellites:

> Jamming of satellite communications can block the main channel of information flow. The enemy's naval force and its national military command authorities, naval command centers and other force links mainly rely on high frequency satellite communications and microwave communications, and all satellite communications, including commercial and military satellite communications, are easily susceptible to electronic interference and deception. In regards to this point, against the transmitters of high frequency satellites used by large naval forces, we can use ground-based high powered satellite communication jammers or vessels installed with high frequency satellite communication jammers to enter into an advantageous position within the wave shape coverage of the communication satellite transmitter and then jam the satellites transmitter at its source and ruin its normal operation and to interrupt the satellite communication with the outside. We can also deploy electronic interference aircraft carrying interference equipment to conduct suppression or deception at the source against ship-borne WSC-3 high frequency communication satellite receivers and SSR-1 satellite signal receivers.[56]

In addition to these measures, radars could be jammed or destroyed, and GPS signals could be jammed.[57]

---

[55] Nie Yubao (聶玉宝), "Electronic Warfare Methods to Attack Large Enemy Ships (打击海上敌大船艇编队的电子战战法)," in Military Studies Editorial Department, *Research on Our Army's Information Warfare Issues* (我军信息战问题研究), Beijing: National Defense University Press, 1999, p. 185.

[56] Nie (1999), pp. 185–186.

[57] Nie (1999), pp. 186–187.

Information warfare tactics are also emphasized in another text on naval warfare, which advocates attacking the command and control functions of a naval group:

> Modern navies are very maneuverable, reflecting high speed and a strong defense. Therefore, their strike needs require a large investment. At the same time, their equipment is highly automated, the technology complex, and the links between their weapons and equipment are difficult to repair once they are damaged. Therefore, there are existing weaknesses. If a strike can be carried out that severely damages a crucial point, it can greatly reduce the operational effectiveness of the target in a short period of time and even basically paralyze them and [cause them to] lose their combat ability and in a short period of time achieve good results. Based on the above situation, in order to overcome insufficiencies in force, the campaign commander when determining which targets to destroy should at an early period take as the main targets paralyzing the enemy's force and destroying the enemy's command capability.[58]

This theme was echoed in a January 2003 *Modern Weaponry* article concerning attacks on Aegis-equipped destroyers. This article, which was described as the author's own opinion, advocated the use of large numbers (54) of Harpy UAVs as anti-radiation drones that would crash into the radars of the destroyers. These attacks would be backed up by anti-radiation missiles launched from Su-30 aircraft. After the radars were disabled, additional Su-30s and *Kilo*-class submarines and *Sovremenny* destroyers could be used to sink the ships.[59]

Space Warfare

Space warfare has recently received an increasing amount of attention from Chinese military writers. The U.S. military's use of space for strategic reconnaissance, communications, navigation and positioning, and early warning has highlighted the importance of space as a force multiplier. In part, based on these observations, Chinese writers

---

[58] Chen Fangyou (1991), pp. 221–222.

[59] "Blockade and Kill Taiwan Independence's 'Aegis'," *Xiandai Bingqi*, January 2, 2003.

have predicted space power to develop as air power has developed, from a reconnaissance force into a strategic bombing force. Because of this, space is thought to be the next "strategic vantage point" from which the control of the air, land, and sea will be determined. According to this logic, the importance of seizing control in space in future battles makes space warfare inevitable. PLA strategists envision the possible expansion of electronic warfare into outer space in future conflicts: "As a result of the continuous development of space technology, military satellites will provide increasingly powerful command and control capabilities in future wars. Thus, it is possible that military satellites will become targets for attack in electronic warfare and that space electronic warfare will become a new field of electronic warfare."[60]

Moreover, many PLA writers have concluded that U.S. space-based systems are vulnerable to attack. A *Liberation Army Daily* article states:

> Currently, space systems have increasingly become systems in which countries' key interests lie. If an anti-satellite weapon destroys a space system in a future war, the destruction will have dealt a blow to the side that owns and uses the space system, stripped it of space supremacy, and weakened its supremacy in conducting information warfare, and even its supremacy in the war at large. Anti-satellite weapons that can be developed at low cost and that can strike at the enemy's enormously expensive yet vulnerable space system will become an important option for the majority of medium-sized and small countries with fragile space technology.[61]

A Xinhua article reiterates this sentiment: "For countries that can never win a war with the United States by using the method of tanks and planes, attacking the U.S. space system may be an irresistible and

---

[60] Peng and Yao (2001), p. 363.

[61] Li Hechun and Chen Yourong, "Sky War: A New Form of War That Might Erupt in the Future," *Liberation Army Daily* (online), January 17, 2001.

most tempting choice."[62] Moreover, one PLA source states that during the Gulf War, 90 percent of strategic communications was handled by satellites, including commercial satellites.[63] From the Chinese perspective, successfully attacking U.S. space-based communication systems could have a powerful impact on the ability of the United States to communicate with forces in a given theater of operations.

Attacks against satellites can be accomplished through the use of soft- and hard-kill methods. Examples of soft-kill methods include jamming, while hard-kill methods include a whole range of anti-satellite technology, such as missiles, directed energy weapons, and antisatellite satellites. Chinese writings on antisatellite operations are generally circumspect, however, especially in relation to hard kills. Although no one method is valued more than another, Chinese writings on space do suggest a desire to develop antisatellite weapons.

One article notes, however, that although China's aerospace industry has built a solid foundation, "it is still far from meeting the requirements for winning a local war under high-technology conditions."[64] Its authors state:

In the future, space military systems will directly participate in local wars that break out around our periphery, including space information support and even offensive and defensive countermeasures. In facing this threat, we should concentrate on intensifying research into the crucial technologies of land-based and space-based (concentrating on space-based) anti-satellite weapons and as soon as possible develop one or two anti-satellite weapons that can threaten the enemy's space systems and seize the initiative in future space wars.[65]

---

[62] Wang Hucheng, "The U.S. Military's Soft Ribs and Strategic Weaknesses," Xinhua, July 5, 2000.

[63] Dai (1999), p. 350.

[64] Xie Yonggao (谢永高), Qin Zizeng (秦子增), and Huang Haibing (黄海兵), "Looking at the Past and Future of Military Aerospace Technology" (军事航天技术的回顾与展望), China Aerospace (中国航天), No. 6, 2002.

[65] Xie, Qin, and Huang (2005).

While Chinese writers do discuss attacking satellites, there is no direct evidence as to what types of space targets the PLA may consider the most important. Chinese authors do not assign a relative value to satellites and instead list all types of satellites as potential targets. Chinese sources on strategy and information warfare, however, provide some clues as to what types of targets may be considered most valuable. As detailed earlier, *Science of Campaigns* lists five key types of targets. Assuming that this list is prioritized, Chinese strategy would seem to value the destruction of intelligence-gathering satellites, which would belong to the second category—"information systems"—over other types of satellites, such as communication and GPS satellites that provide links between various campaign systems and therefore fall into the fifth category.

This prioritization is also supported by various writings on information warfare. In these writings, information collection is regarded as the basis of information warfare. One source states, "First, the direct goal and basis of operations to achieve campaign information control is the collection of information and the maintaining of information superiority."[66] In fact, another source describes "intelligence warfare" as the primary operational method and asserts that whoever achieves intelligence superiority will be able to achieve a high degree of battlefield transparency, which could then lead to seizing operational initiative and winning the war.[67] Another source goes further by describing intelligence warfare as holding a "special position" in the realm of information countermeasures:

> "Know the enemy and know yourself and you can fight a hundred battles without defeat." Under information warfare conditions, only by having clear intelligence on the enemy and the operational area and even the enemy's country, and by strictly

---

[66] Zhang Jianhong (张建洪), "Operations to Achieve Campaign Information Control" (夺取战役制信息权作战探要), in Military Studies Editorial Department, *Research on Our Army's Information Warfare Issues*, Beijing: National Defense University Press, 1999, p. 68.

[67] Lu Daohai (鲁道海), *Information Operations: Exploring the Seizure of Information Control* (信息作战夺取制信息权的探索), Beijing: Junshi Yiwen Press (军事谊文出版社), 1999, p. 74.

controlling our intelligence, can correct judgments of the battle-field be made, correct operational guidance given, and information attacks and firepower attacks correctly organized to paralyze enemy operational systems and maintain the concealment of operational movement in order to accomplish campaign goals.[68]

Perhaps because intelligence collection forms the basis of information superiority, one source states, "before an operation, or in the opening stages of an operation, enemy reconnaissance and early warning systems must be struck."[69] This statement is echoed in another source, which states, "When a campaign starts, the main tasks of an information operation are to attack enemy reconnaissance systems and implement campaign information deception to conceal our operational intent and protect the start of our campaign force."[70]

Other types of satellites, however, have also been discussed as targets. Considering the PLA's emphasis on attacking command and control targets, it is not surprising that attacking communication satellites has been discussed. One source states:

> Jamming satellite communications can block the main channel of information flow. The enemy's naval force and its national military command authorities, naval command centers and other force links mainly rely on high frequency satellite communications and microwave communications and all other satellite communications, including commercial and military satellite communications, all of which are easily susceptible to electronic interference and deception. In regards to this point, we can use ground-based high-powered satellite communication jammers or vessels installed with high frequency satellite communication

---

[68] Xu Yuanxian (徐源先), "Future Basic Methods of Our Army's Information Warfare" (试论未来我军信息战的基本样式), in Military Studies Editorial Department, *Research on Our Army's Information Warfare Issues*, Beijing: National Defense University Press (国防大学出版社), 1999, p. 29.

[69] Wang Huying (王沪鹰), "The Basic Principles and Campaign Methods of Information Attacks" (信息进攻的基本原则激战法), in Military Studies Editorial Department, *Research on Our Army's Information Warfare Issues*, Beijing: National Defense University Press, 1999, p. 82.

[70] Dai (1999), p. 313.

jammers against the transmitters of high frequency satellites used by large naval forces in order to enter into an advantageous position within the wave shape coverage of the communication satellite transmitter. We can then jam the satellite's transmitter at its source, destroying its normal operation and interrupting satellite communication with the outside. We can also deploy electronic interference aircraft to conduct suppression or deception at the source against ship-borne WSC-3 high frequency communication satellite receivers and SSR-1 satellite signal receivers.[71]

In addition, because of the United States' reliance on satellite positioning for targeting, the U.S. GPS system may also be a target. A *Liberation Army Daily* article outlines three vulnerabilities of the GPS system. First, it notes, the GPS signal can be easily jammed by signals produced by commercial television stations, satellite communications, and mobile satellite terminals.[72] Another method is to use space-based jammers to disrupt the GPS signal at its source.[73] Second, altering the signal to avoid jamming is difficult and would have negative consequences for global transportation. Finally, GPS satellites are vulnerable to direct attack.[74] Another *Liberation Army Daily* article states that "the optimal method for dealing with coordinate warfare is to destroy the opposition's NAVSTAR satellites or to use the same coordinate warfare methods to counter attack the opposition's vital targets."[75] But jamming the GPS signal does not need to be complex. It is reportedly inexpensive and can be purchased with off-the-shelf

---

[71] Nie (1999), p. 185.

[72] Shi Chunmin, "War Is Aimed at the Soft Rib of GPS, (战争瞄向GPS '软肋')," *Liberation Army Daily* (online), January 15, 2003.

[73] Zhu Rinzhong, "The Theory of GPS and Methods of Countering It," *Junshi Xueshu*, May 1999; Dean Cheng, "The Chinese Space Program: A 21st Century Fleet in Being," in James C. Mulvenon and Andrew N.D. Yang, *A Poverty of Riches: New Challenges and Opportunities in PLA Research*, Santa Monica, Calif.: RAND Corporation, CF-189-NSRD, 2003, p. 46. Interfering with a GPS signal involves jamming the GPS receivers, not transmitters. In this case, the author is advocating an ill-advised tactic.

[74] Shi (2003).

[75] Liu Sunshan, "Military Experts Believe That Coordinate War Is Coming onto the Warfare Stage," *Liberation Army Daily*, June 13, 2001.

technology for less than $400.[76] China may also be less inclined to discriminate in its GPS jamming. According to one article:

> To low-tech rivals such as countries that do not rely heavily on GPS, in particular, it is not necessary to worry about the consequences of one's jamming, nor is it necessary to select the frequency and scope of interference, which do not have simple counter measures. In contrast, for countries highly reliant on GPS, it is necessary to limit their jamming power to a narrow, specific scope of frequency from a long distance, but the control and focus of this kind of jamming power is relatively difficult.[77]

Conclusion

In a high-tech local war contingency, the PLA would initially not engage an adversary in a traditional force-on-force showdown. The PLA would instead seek to determine an enemy's center of gravity and then attack those key points that paralyze enemy operations or produce opportunities that can be decisively exploited. This strategy is evident in the two types of operations examined in this chapter. When attacking CVBGs, PLA strategists do not consider the aircraft carrier to be the preliminary target. Instead, PLA forces would first attack the battle group's information systems. In the case of airborne assets, AWACS (Airborne Warning and Control System) planes would be attacked first to blind the battle group, and in the case of surface assets, PLA strategists envision attacking Aegis-equipped ships to knock out their powerful radar. This tactic paves the way for follow-on attacks by aircraft, ships, or submarines that would then target the aircraft carrier.

In regard to attacks against U.S. space assets, Chinese authors recognize the growing importance of the use of space in U.S. military

---

[76] Liu Weiguo, "The Soft Rib of the High Technology Battlefield: GPS" (现代高技术战场软肋: GPS)," *Liberation Army Daily* (online), July 18, 2001.

[77] Liu Weiguo (2001).

operations and its vulnerability to attack. This belief has led many writers in the Chinese space community to advocate developing anti-satellite weapons and suggest that the PLA may attack U.S. space assets to deny the U.S. military the use of critical C4ISR assets.

How well the PLA may be able to carry out these attacks is uncertain, though progress is being made. In regard to naval operations, Chinese strategy emphasizes the use of submarines and air assets rather than surface forces. The PLAN has approximately 60 attack submarines that could be used to attack CVBG. In addition, the PLA has approximately 3,200 combat-capable aircraft of which about 150 are considered fourth-generation fighters. The PLA could be expected to use its fourth-generation fighters as a vanguard force to strike vulnerabilities and use the large numbers of less advanced aircraft to exploit successes.

Finding and successfully attacking a CVBG, however, may be a difficult task for the PLA. It does have satellites, OTH radar, and airborne reconnaissance assets, including UAVs, that could be used to locate a CVBG. How well these systems function in practice and the survivability of airborne assets and OTH radar is unknown. Another important consideration is training. Attacking CVBGs would require a complex set of coordinated actions that may be beyond the realm of current PLA capability.

These factors are further compounded by the training and technology of the opponent. If the PLA were unable to "blind" U.S. forces by successfully attacking its C4ISR systems, these types of attacks would be vulnerable to U.S. NCW strategies. The U.S. Navy honed its skills to defend CVBGs during the Cold War with sophisticated "cat and mouse" operations against the Soviet Navy involving advanced technological countermeasures. Any CVBG could thus be expected to offer a stiff defense against any type of PLA attack and with the likelihood of catching the U.S. Navy unaware remote, the PLA's advantage would be extremely limited.

While successfully attacking a CVBG would be difficult for the PLA, the U.S. military can take steps now to further reduce the threat. Considering the large number of PLA submarines and the importance the PLA places on subsurface operations, the U.S. Navy may need to reemphasize antisubmarine warfare training. In addition, the U.S. Navy may also need to consider how best to defend surface ships against mass attacks from manned aircraft or UAVs armed with antiship cruise missiles, or UAVs designed to crash into warships. Finally, enhancing NCW capabilities may allow the Navy to detect and take defensive measures before an adversary can take action.

In regard to counter-space operations, China is believed to be conducting research and development on a number of different anti-satellite weapons, including direct-ascent systems, antisatellite satellites, radio frequency weapons, and lasers. The ability to operate these types of systems would imperil all or some types of U.S. space-based assets whose destruction, denial, or degradation could reduce the ability of the U.S. military to conduct NCW. While space-based assets may be viewed as easy targets, the consequences of engaging in active space warfare operations against U.S. space forces may also limit PLA capabilities. In response to an attack against its space assets, the U.S. military could attack China's space assets to degrade the PLA's communications and information-gathering capabilities. Attacking the GPS constellation may also deny GPS to PLA forces, although access to a Chinese satellite navigation system[78] or to the planned European Galileo system may ameliorate this concern. Attacking satellites that are operated or used by multiple countries may also draw other countries into the conflict and may sway international opinion against it.

Despite these concerns, the growing importance of space to U.S. operations may make them an irresistible target. The more the U.S. military relies on space for critical operational support, the more U.S. operations will be exposed to a debilitating attack in space. Consequently, the U.S. military may need to take steps before a conflict arises to prepare for any contingency. Technologies may need to be developed and made operational to detect, defend, and harden satellites against attack. The U.S. military may also need to improve its ability to replace satellites by increasing launch capabilities and hav-

---

[78] China now has three "Beidou" (Big Dipper) navigation and positioning satellites in orbit that provide coverage to China and the surrounding region.

ing a reserve of satellites. A robust defense against attacks on space assets may also need to consider attacks against Chinese launch facilities, which would require operations deep into Chinese territory.

The nature of the Chinese threat presented in this chapter requires the U.S. military to operate in different ways than it has in operations since 1991. Unlike recent opponents, the PLA is developing strategies and technologies to defeat the U.S. technological advantage. Consequently, to prepare for a conflict with China, the U.S. military must begin to emphasize defensive training and technologies. This may require the U.S. military to emphasize defensive operations rather than focus on naval aviation in the ground attack role or to leave space assets undefended.

CHAPTER FIVE

Option Two: Subversion, Sabotage, and Information Operations

In the minds of the Chinese leadership, the available evidence suggests that the most important political-military challenge and the most likely flashpoint for Sino-U.S. conflict is Taiwan. In seeking to reunify the island with the mainland, however, it is important to note that China has a political strategy with a military component, not a military strategy with a political component. China would prefer to win without fighting, since its worst-case outcome is a failed operation that would result in de facto independence for Taiwan. Also, the leadership realizes that attacking Taiwan with kinetic weapons would result in significant international opprobrium and make the native population ungovernable. These assumptions explain why China, until recently, maintained a "wait and see" attitude toward Taiwan, even though the island elected a president from a party committed previously to independence. From 2000 until late 2003, China eschewed saber rattling in favor of economic enticement and "united front" cooperation with the Pan-Blue opposition, both of which were believed to be working successfully. In November 2003, in response to perceived provocations by Taiwan President Chen Shui-bian, Beijing once again revived the threat of military force to deter what it saw as further slippage toward independence, dramatically increasing tensions in the U.S.-China-Taiwan triangle.

Should the situation deteriorate into direct military conflict, the PLA, since 1992, has been hard at work bolstering the hedging options of the leadership, developing advanced campaign doctrines, testing the concepts in increasingly complex training and exercises, and integrating new indigenous and imported weapon systems. At the strategic level, the writings of Chinese military authors suggest that there are two main centers of gravity in a Taiwan scenario. The first of these is the will of the Taiwanese people, which they hope to undermine through exercises, missile attacks, special operations, and other operations that have a psychological-operation focus. Based on assessments of the 1995–1996 exercises, as well as public opinion polling in Taiwan, China appears to have concluded that the Taiwanese people do not have the stomach for conflict and would therefore sue for peace after suffering only a small amount of pain. The second center of gravity is the will and capability of the United States to intervene decisively in a cross-Strait conflict. In a strategic sense, China has traditionally believed that its intercontinental ballistic missile (ICBM) inventory, which is capable of striking CONUS, will serve as a deterrent to U.S. intervention, or at least a brake on escalation. Closer to Taiwan, the PLA has been engaged in an active program of equipment modernization, purchasing niche anti-access, area-denial capabilities such as long-range cruise missiles and submarines to shape the operational calculus of the American CVBG commander on station. At the same time, a key lesson learned from analyzing U.S. military operations since Operation Desert Storm was the vulnerability of the logistics and deployment system.

Center of Gravity Number One:
The Will of the People on Taiwan

Chinese strategies to manipulate the national psychology of the populace and leadership on Taiwan involve the full spectrum of information operations, including psychological operations, special operations, computer network operations, and intelligence operations. To this end, Beijing can employ all of the social, economic, political, and military tools of Chinese national power, as well as enlist the assistance of private-sector players and sympathetic co-conspirators on Taiwan. The goal of these efforts is to shake the widely perceived psychological fragility of the populace, causing the government to prematurely capitulate to political negotiations with the mainland. In a sense, China seeks to use the immaturity of Taiwanese democracy against itself.

Analysis in this chapter of both Beijing's strategies in this arena as well as Taipei's ability to resist such methods strongly suggests Taiwan's high-level vulnerability to Chinese soft coercion and raises major questions about the island's viability in the opening phase of a Chinese coercion campaign, their credibility as a source of intelligence information on the mainland and a keeper of U.S. secrets, and their expected ability to interoperate successfully with U.S. forces in a crisis.

Taiwan's vulnerabilities in the critical infrastructure protection arena can be divided into two categories: informational and physical. On the information side, Taiwan is a highly information-dependent society with a relatively low level of information or computer security. Significant disruptions in information systems could have major negative effects on the island, particularly in the economic and financial realms, thus increasing fear and panic among the population. Past Chinese uses of regional media to send psychological operations messages have also enjoyed success in affecting popular morale and public opinion. For example, an Internet rumor in 1999 that a Chinese Su-27 had shot down a Taiwan aircraft caused the Taipei stock market to drop more than 2 percent in less than four hours.

On the physical side of the equation, Taiwan's current capability and readiness level is much lower than one might expect for a state under such a direct level of threat, especially when compared with other "national security states" like Israel or South Korea. Critical infrastructure protection has been a low priority for the government, and Taiwan is acutely vulnerable to Spetnaz-like or fifth-column operations, aided significantly by ethnic and linguistic homogeneity and significant cross-border flows, which facilitate entry and access to potential targets. In terms of civilian infrastructure, Taiwan's telecommunications, electric power, and transportation infrastructure are all highly susceptible to sabotage. These weaknesses have been indirectly exposed by periodic natural disasters, such as the September

1999 earthquake and the September 2001 typhoon, when the communications infrastructure effectively collapsed. Taiwan's ports, including Su'ao, Jeelung, and Gaoxiong (the third highest volume container port in the world), are attractive targets. Port charts and ship movements are available on the Internet, and Gaoxiong in particular has two narrow mouths that could easily be blocked with scuttled vessels. Taiwan's highways are a vulnerable bottleneck, particularly given the large number of undefended mountain tunnels and bridges that could be destroyed by special operations units. Finally, the power grid is known to be fragile, marked by numerous single-point failure nodes and no cross-hatching of sub-grids to form redundancy. The loss of a single tower in the central mountainous region, thanks to a landslide, knocked out 90 percent of the grid a couple of years ago, and delays in construction of a fourth nuclear plant have constrained capacity.

Special operations forces and fifth column are also a major threat for disruption of military command and control and decapitation of the national command authority, as well as providing reconnaissance for initial missile and air strikes and battle damage assessments for follow-on strikes. Entry into the country for special operations forces is not a substantial obstacle, thanks to ethnic and linguistic homogeneity and the dramatic increases in cross-Strait people flows. Between 1988 and October 2002, for example, more than 828,000 mainlanders visited the island. Moreover, these special forces could also facilitate control of key civilian and military airfields and ports that could be used as points of entry for invading forces. The lack of operational security at key facilities is particularly inexplicable and appalling. Visits to national political and military command centers reveal them to be relatively unguarded with poor information security practices, including the use of personal cell phones in supposedly secure areas. The presidential palace in downtown Taipei, home to the president and his key staff, has no fence line and no security checkpoints. Building information, including the location of the president's office, is openly available on the Internet. Given the poor performance of President Chen's personal security detail during the recent assassination attempt on his life, the possibility of elimination of the top leadership through direct action cannot be discounted. Finally, there is substantial open source evidence to suggest that China is winning the intelligence war across the Strait, raising serious doubts about the purity of Taiwanese intelligence proffered to the United States, the safety of advanced military technologies transferred to the island, and the ability of official Taiwan interlocutors to safeguard shared U.S. secrets about intelligence collection or joint war-planning. In the past five years, a steady series of leaked stories have appeared in Taiwan's and other regional media, describing either the rounding up of Taiwanese agent networks on the mainland or the unmasking of high-ranking Taiwanese agents in the military, with similar successes a rarity on the Taiwan side, despite significant political incentive to publicize such discoveries.[1] Reported examples since only early 2003 include the arrest of the president of the PLA Air Force Command Academy, Major-General Liu Guangzhi, his former deputy, Major-General Li Suolin, and 10 of their subordinates;[2] the arrest of 24 Taiwanese and 19 mainlanders in late 2003;[3] the arrest of

---

[1] Among the rare examples, which perversely strengthen the case for significant counter-intelligence concerns on Taiwan, are three military officers (Maj. Pai Chin-yang, Tseng Chao-wen and Chen Sui-chiung) arrested for spying and two individuals (Huang Cheng-an and his girlfriend) arrested for transferring technology from the Chungshan Institute for Science and Technology to the mainland. See William Foreman, "Taiwan Arrests Military Officer on Spy Charges—The Third Such Case in Month," Associated Press, December 3, 2003, and "Taiwan Detains Woman Over Alleged Spying," *South China Morning Post*, January 30, 2004. An earlier case also involved Yeh Yu-chen and Chen Shih-liang and technology from the Chungshan Institute. See "Taiwan Attempts Damage-Control After Alleged Chinese Spy Ring," Agence France-Presse, August 7, 2003.

[2] "Top PLA Officers Accused of Spying for Taiwan," *Straits Times*, April 16, 2004; "Beijing Arrests Military Officers on Spy Charges," *China Post*, April 17, 2004.

[3] The timing and propaganda exploitation of the arrests, which coincided with the Taiwan presidential campaign, suggests that the Chinese already had the individuals under surveillance and chose to arrest them for maximum political effect. See Philip P. Pan, "China Arrests 43 Alleged Spies; Move Increases Effort to Undermine Taiwanese President," *Washington Post*, December 24, 2003; "Chinese Mainland Smashes Taiwan Spy Ring," Xinhua, December 24, 2003; "Espionage, Corruption Cases in China, Dec 03–Feb 04," *BBC Monitoring International Reports*, February 14, 2004; Joe McDonald, "China Parades Accused Taiwanese Spies in Front of Cameras Amid Tensions with Island," Associated Press, January 16, 2004; and "Taiwan Spies Visited by Families," Xinhua, January 20, 2004.

Chang Hsu-min, 27, and his 24-year-old girlfriend Yu Shi-ping;[4] the arrest of Xu Jianchi;[5] the arrest of Ma Peiming in February 2003;[6] and the arrest and conviction to life imprisonment of Petty Officer First Class Liu Yueh-lung for passing naval communications codes to China.[7] Farther back, high-profile intelligence losses include the discovery, arrest, and executions of General Logistics Department Lieutenant-General Liu Liankun and Senior Colonel Shao Zhengzhong as a result of Taiwanese government intelligence disclosures about the fact that warheads on Chinese missiles fired near the island in 1996 were unarmed;[8] the arrest and sentencing of Hainan Province deputy head Lin Kecheng and nine others in 1999 for providing economic, political, and other kinds of intelligence to the Taiwan Military Intelligence Bureau;[9] and the arrest and imprisonment of a local official in Nanchong, Sichuan, named Wang Ping for allegedly also working for the MIB.[10] In addition, retired senior Taiwan intelligence officials, including National Security Bureau personnel chief Pan Hsi-hsien and at least one former J-2, continue to travel to and often residence in China despite Taiwan regulations barring such movement for three years after retirement.[11] At the same time, Taiwan and international media are regularly filled with purported leaks about sensitive U.S.-Taiwan military interactions or weapon transfers, sourced to either legislators or standing Taiwan government officials. Examples include disclosures alleging the possible deployment of an Integrated Underwater Surveillance System north and south of the island to detect

---

[4] "China Detains Two More Taiwanese Suspected of Espionage," Agence France-Presse, February 13, 2004 [citing Chinese state media].

[5] *Chongqing Ribao*, August 8, 2003, p. 1.

[6] Agence France-Presse, September 2, 2003, p. 1.

[7] Brian Hsu, "Petty Officer Gets Life Sentence," *Taipei Times Online*, December 18, 2002.

[8] John Pomfret, "Taiwanese Mistake Led to 3 Spies' Executions," *Washington Post*, February 20, 2000.

[9] *People's Daily* article in August 1999, cited in Pomfret (2000).

[10] Sichuan television report in October 1999, cited in Pomfret (2000).

[11] "Former Taiwan Spy Chief Denies Leaking Secrets During His Four Years in China," *TaiwanNews.com* (Associated Press), April 14, 2004.

Chinese submarines,[12] the reported provision of early warning data on Chinese missile attack from the Defense Support Program satellite constellation,[13] and the alleged SIGINT cooperation between the National Security Agency and Taiwan on Yangming Mountain.[14] All of these possible compromises raise serious concerns about future technology or information sharing with Taiwan.

Center of Gravity Number Two: U.S. Military Intervention

Strategies for Attacking U.S. Logistics

When Chinese strategists contemplate how to affect U.S. deployments, they confront the limitations of their current conventional force, which does not have range sufficient to interdict U.S. facilities or assets beyond the Japanese home islands. Nuclear options, while theoretically available, are nonetheless far too escalatory to be used so early in the conflict. Theater missile systems, which are possibly moving to a mixture of conventional and nuclear warheads, could be used against Japan or Guam, but uncertainties about the nature of a given warhead would likely generate responses similar to the nuclear scenario.

According to the predictable cadre of "true believers," both of the centers of gravity identified above can be attacked using computer network operations (CNO). In the first case, the Chinese information operations (IO) community believes that CNO will play a useful psychological role in undermining the will of the Taiwanese people by attacking infrastructure and economic vitality. In the second case, the Chinese IO community envisions CNO effectively deterring or

---

[12] Michael Gordon, "Secret U.S. Study Concludes Taiwan Needs New Arms," *New York Times*, April 1, 2001.

[13] "US to Share Early-Warning Missile Data With Taiwan," Agence France-Presse, October 8, 2002.

[14] Wendell Minnick, "Taiwan-USA Link Up on SIGINT," *Jane's Defense Review*, January 23, 2001; Wendell Minnick, "Spook Mountain: How US Spies on China," *Asia Times Online*, March 6, 2003; and Wendell Minnick, "Challenge to Update Taiwan's SIGINT," *Jane's Intelligence Review*, February 1, 2004.

delaying U.S. intervention and causing pain sufficient to compel Taipei to capitulate before the United States arrives. The remainder of this section outlines how these IO theorists propose operationalizing such a strategy.

General IO and CNA Analysis

Before examining this scenario in detail, it is first necessary to provide some background regarding Chinese views of information operations in general, and computer network operations in particular. At the strategic level, contemporary writers view IO and CNO as useful supplements to conventional warfighting capability and powerful asymmetric options for "overcoming the superior with the inferior." According to one Chinese author, "computer network attack is one of the most effective means for a weak military to fight a strong one."[15] Yet another important theme in Chinese writings on CNO is the use of CNA as the spear point of deterrence. Emphasizing the potential role of CNA in this type of signaling, a Chinese strategist writes that "We must send a message to the enemy through computer network attack, forcing the enemy to give up without fighting."[16] CNA is particularly attractive to the PLA, since it has a longer range than its conventional power projection assets. This allows the PLA to "reach out and touch" the United States, even as far as CONUS. "Thanks to computers," one strategist writes, "long-distance surveillance and accurate, powerful and long-distance attacks are now available to our military."[17] Yet CNA is also believed to enjoy a high degree of "plausible deniability," rendering it a possible tool of strategic denial and deception. As one source notes, "An information war is inexpensive, as the enemy country can receive a paralyzing blow through the

---

[15] *Campaign Studies*, pp. 173–174.

[16] Nu Li, Li Jiangzhou, and Xu Dehui, "Strategies in Information Operations: A Preliminary Discussion," *Military Science*, Vol. 13, No. 2, April 2000.

[17] *Campaign Studies*, p. 170.

Internet, and the party on the receiving end will not be able to tell whether it is a child's prank or an attack from an enemy."[18]

It is important to note that Chinese CNA doctrine focuses on disruption and paralysis, not destruction. Philosophically and historically, the evolving doctrine draws inspiration from Mao Zedong's theory of "protracted war," in which he argued that "we must as far as possible seal up the enemies' eyes and ears, and make them become blind and deaf, and we must as far as possible confuse the minds of their commanders and turn them into madmen, using this to achieve our own victory."[19] One authoritative source states: "computer warfare targets computers—the core of weapons systems and C4I systems—in order to paralyze the enemy."[20] The goal of this paralyzing attack is to inflict a "mortal blow" [*zhiming daji* 致命打击], though this does not necessarily refer to defeat. Instead, Chinese analysts often speak of using these attacks to deter the enemy or to raise the costs of conflict to an unacceptable level. Specifically, CNA on non-military targets are designed to "...shake war resoluteness, destroy war potential and win the upper hand in war," thus undermining the political will of the population for participation in military conflict.[21]

At an operational level, the emerging Chinese IO strategy has five key features. First, Chinese authors emphasize defense as the top priority and chastise American theorists for their "fetish of the offensive." In interviews, analysts assert their belief that the United States is already carrying out extensive computer network exploitation (CNE) activities against Chinese servers. As a result, computer network defense must be the highest priority in peacetime, and only after that problem is solved can they consider "tactical counter-offensives." Second, information warfare is viewed as an unconventional warfare weapon to be used in the opening phase of the conflict,

---

[18] Wei Jincheng, "New Form of People's War," *Jiefangjun bao,* June 25, 1996, p. 6.

[19] Mao Zedong, "On Protracted War" (May 1938), in *Selected Works of Mao Zedong*, Vol. II, Beijing: Foreign Languages Press, 1961, paragraph 83.

[20] *Information Operations,* p. 288.

[21] *Information Operations,* p. 296.

not a battlefield force multiplier that can be employed during every phase of the war. PLA analysts believe that a bolt from the blue at the beginning is necessary, because the enemy may simply unplug the network, denying access to the target set, or patch the relevant vulnerabilities, thus obviating all prior intelligence preparation of the battlefield. Third, information warfare is seen as a tool to permit China to fight and win an information campaign, precluding the need for conventional military action. Fourth, China's enemies, in particular the United States, are seen as "information dependent," while China is not. This latter point is an interesting misperception, given that the current Chinese C4I modernization is paradoxically making China more vulnerable to U.S. methods.

Perhaps most significant, CNA is characterized as a preemption weapon to be used under the rubric of the rising Chinese strategy of *xianfa zhiren,* or "gaining mastery before the enemy has struck." Preemption [*xianfa zhiren* 先发制人] is a core concept of emerging Chinese military doctrine. One author recommends that an effective strategy by which the weaker party can overcome its more powerful enemy is "to take advantage of serious gaps in the deployment of forces by the enemy with a high tech edge by launching a preemptive strike during the early phase of the war or in the preparations leading to the offensive."[22] Confirming earlier analysis of Chinese views of U.S. operational vulnerabilities in the deployment phase, the reason for striking is that the "enemy is most vulnerable during the early phase of the war."[23] In terms of specific targets, the author asserts that "we should zero in on the hubs and other crucial links in the system that moves enemy troops as well as the war-making machine, such as harbors, airports, means of transportation, battlefield installations, and the communications, command and control and information systems."[24] If these targets are not attacked or the attack fails, the "high-tech equipped enemy" will amass troops and deploy hardware

---

[22] Lu Linzhi (1996).

[23] Lu Linzhi (1996).

[24] Lu Linzhi (1996).

swiftly to the war zone, where it will carry out "large-scale airstrikes in an attempt to weaken...China's combat capability."[25] More recent and authoritative sources expand on this view. "In order to control information power," one source states, "there must also be preemption...information offensives mainly rely on distant battle and stealth in order to be effective, and are best used as a surprise... Therefore, it is clear that whoever strikes first has the advantage."[26] "The best defense is offense," according to the authors of *Information Operations*. "We must launch preemptive attacks to disrupt and destroy enemy computer systems."[27]

Specific Targeting Analysis of Network Attacks Against Logistics

There are two macro-level targets for Chinese computer network operations: military network information and military information stored on networks. CNA seeks to use the former to degrade the latter. Like U.S. doctrine, Chinese CNA targeting focuses specifically on "enemy C2 centers," especially "enemy information systems." Of these information systems, PLA writings and interviews suggest that logistics computer systems are a top military target. According to one PLA source, "we must zero in on the...crucial links in the system that move enemy troops... such as information systems."[28] Another source writes, "we must attack system information accuracy, timeliness of information, and reliability of information."[29] In addition to logistics computer systems, another key military target for Chinese CNA is military reliance on civilian communications systems.

These concepts, combined with the earlier analysis of the PLA view that the main U.S. weakness is the deployment phase, lead PLA IO theorists to conclude that U.S. dependence on computer systems, particularly logistics systems, is a weak link that could potentially be

---

[25] Lu Linzhi (1996).

[26] *Campaign Studies*, pp. 178–179.

[27] *Information Operations*, p. 324.

[28] Lu Linzhi (1996).

[29] *Information Operations*, p. 293.

exploited through CNA. Specifically, Chinese authors highlight DoD's need to use the civilian backbone and unclassified computer networks (e.g., NIPRNET [Non-Secure Internet Protocol Router Network]) as an Achilles' heel. There is also recognition of the fact that operations in the Pacific are especially reliant on precisely co-ordinated transportation, communications, and logistics networks, given the "tyranny of distance" in the theater. PLA strategists believe that a disruptive CNA against these systems or affiliated civilian systems could potentially delay or degrade U.S. force deployment to the region while allowing China to maintain a degree of plausible deniability.

The Chinese are right to highlight the NIPRNET as an attractive *and* accessible target, unlike its classified counterparts. It is attractive because it contains and transmits critical deployment information in the all-important TPFDL (time-phased force deployment list), which is valuable for intelligence gathering about U.S. military operations as well as a lucrative target for disruptive attacks. In terms of accessibility, it was relatively easy to gather data about the NIRPNET from open sources, at least prior to 9/11. Moreover, the very nature of the system is the source of its vulnerabilities, since it has to be unclassified and connected to the greater global network, albeit through protected gateways. To migrate all of the NIPRNET to a secure, air-gapped network would likely tax the resources and bandwidth of DoD's military networks.

DoD's classified networks are an attractive but less accessible target for the Chinese. On the one hand, these networks would be an intelligence gold mine and are likely a priority CNE target. On the other hand, they are a less attractive CNA target, thanks to the difficulty of penetrating its defenses. Any overall Chinese military strategy predicated on a high degree of success in penetrating these networks during crisis or war is a high-risk venture and increases the chances of failure of the overall effort to an unacceptable level. Moreover, internal Chinese writings on information warfare show no confidence in China's ability to get inside NCW aboard deployed ships or other self-contained operational units. Instead, the literature is focused on preventing the units from deploying in the first place and thereafter breaking the C4I linkages between the ships and their headquarters.

Chinese CNE/CNA operations against logistics networks could have a detrimental impact on U.S. logistics support to operations. Chinese CNE activities directed against U.S. military logistics networks could reveal force deployment information, such as the names of ships deployed, readiness status of various units, timing and destination of deployments, and rendezvous schedules. This is especially important for the Chinese in times of crisis, since they utilize U.S. military Web sites and newspapers as principal sources of deployment information in peacetime. An October 2001 *People's Daily* article, for example, explicitly cited U.S. Navy Web sites for information about the origins, destination, and purpose of two CVBGs exercising in the South China Sea. Because the quantity and quality of deployment information on open Web sites has been dramatically reduced after 9/11, the intelligence benefits of exploiting the NIPRNET have become even more paramount.[30] CNA could also delay resupply to the theater by misdirecting stores, fuel, and munitions, corrupting or deleting inventory files, and thereby hindering mission capability.

The advantages to this strategy are numerous: (1) it is available to the PLA in the near term; (2) it does not require the PLA to be able to attack or invade Taiwan with air or sea assets; (3) it has a reasonable level of deniability, provided that the attack is sophisticated enough to prevent tracing; (4) it exploits perceived U.S. casualty aversion, overattention to force protection, the tyranny of distance in the Pacific, and U.S. dependence on information systems; and (5) it could achieve the desired operational and psychological effects: deterrence of U.S. response or degrading of deployments.

---

[30] DoD's revised Web site (1998) administration guidance specifically prohibits the following: "Reference to unclassified information that would reveal sensitive movements of military assets or the location of units, installations, or personnel where uncertainty regarding location is an element of a military plan or program" (3.5.3.2).

Conclusions: Is the Scenario Realistic?

Chinese IO theorists assert that computer networks attacks against unclassified computer systems or affiliated civilian systems, combined with a coordinated campaign of short-range ballistic missile attacks, "fifth column," and information warfare attacks against Taiwanese critical infrastructure, could quickly force Taiwan to capitulate to Beijing. This strategy exploits serious vulnerabilities, particularly with regard to Taiwanese critical infrastructure and U.S. military reliance on the NIPRNET, but it is also partially predicated on a set of mis-understandings, misperceptions, and exaggerations of both U.S. logistics operations and the efficacy of PLA information operations. This final section assesses the balance of these perceptions and mis-perceptions, concluding with an evaluation of the cost-benefit calcu-lus for the PLA in undertaking such an effort.

Chinese Strategies Against U.S. Logistics Systems and Operations

The Chinese are correct to point to the NIPRNET as a potential vul-nerability, but would such an attack actually produce the desired effect? First, there is the issue of the "ready" CVBGs at Yokusuka, which is only a few days steam away from Taiwan. Although extended resupply might be degraded, the group's arrival time would not be heavily affected by attacks on the NIPRNET, undermining a strategic goal of the attacks in the first place. In response, PLA ana-lysts point to times in the past several years when there was no ready carrier in the Pacific because it was "gapped" in the Mediterranean or in the Persian Gulf. More recently, PLA analysts took note of the DoD's formal revision of its strategy from two major theaters of war to one. In both cases, they could envision scenarios in which U.S. forces would require seven or more days to arrive near Taiwan, poten-tially providing China with a "window of opportunity" to carry out rapid coercive operations against Taiwan.

Second, there is the issue of Chinese characterizations of the U.S. logistics system itself. The Chinese tend to overemphasize the United States' reliance on computers. The writings of some Chinese strategists indicate that they believe the U.S. system cannot function effectively without these computer networks. Moreover, Chinese strategists generally underestimate the capacity of the system to use paper, pencil, fax, and phone if necessary. In fact, interviews with current logistics personnel suggest that downtime on these systems is a regular occurrence, forcing U.S. logistics personnel to periodically employ noncomputerized solutions. At the same time, there is also evidence that U.S. logistics systems are moving toward increasing automation, which would increase the potential impact of an attack against the NIPRNET.

Third, Chinese analysis seems predicated on questionable assumptions about American casualty aversion, particularly the notion that U.S. forces would not deploy to a Taiwan contingency until all of the assets were in place. If logistics delays meant that some part of the force protection package would not be available, they assume, then U.S. forces would wait until they arrived before intervening in the conflict. This is a debatable assumption, particularly given the precedence of the two CVBG deployments in 1996 and Washington's considerable interests in the maintenance of peace and stability in the Strait.

Could the Chinese Actually Do It? In terms of courses of action, interviews and internal Chinese writings reveal interest in the full spectrum of CNA tools, including hacking, viruses, physical attack, insider sabotage, and electromagnetic attack. One of the most difficult challenges of this type of analysis is measuring China's actual CNA capability. In rough terms, this type of capability requires four things, three of which are easy to obtain and one of which is harder. The easy three are a computer, an Internet connection, and hacker tools, thousands of which can be downloaded from enthusiast sites around the globe. The more difficult piece of the puzzle to acquire is the operator himself, the computer hacker. While individuals of this ilk are abundant in China's urban centers, they are also correctly perceived to be a social group unlikely to relish military or governmental service.

The answer may be found in the rise of "patriotic hacking" by increasingly sophisticated, nationalistic hacker groups. As demonstrated by the "hacker wars" that followed former Taiwan President

Lee Teng-hui's announcement of "special state-to-state relations," the U.S. bombing of the Chinese embassy in Yugoslavia, and the EP-3 crisis, patriotic hacking appears to have become a permanent feature of Chinese foreign and security policy crises in recent years. On the one hand, the emergence of this trend presents the Chinese military and political leadership with serious command and control problems. Specifically, uncontrolled hacking by irregulars against the United States and Taiwan could potentially undermine a Chinese political-military coercive diplomacy strategy vis-à-vis Taiwan and the United States during a crisis. Unlike traditional military instruments, such as missiles, many of the levers of computer network operations by "unofficial means" are beyond the control of the Chinese government. This could negate the intended impact of strategic pausing and other political signals during a crisis. Yet at the same time patriotic hacking offers several new opportunities for China. First, it increases plausible deniability for official Chinese CNA/CNE. Second, it has the potential to create a large, if unsophisticated, set of operators who could engage in disruption activities against U.S. and Taiwan networks.

For these reasons, some Western analysts have been tempted to assert that the patriotic hackers are "controlled" by Beijing. Among the arguments marshaled to support this thesis is the fact that consistently harsh punishments are meted out to individuals in China committing relatively minor computer crimes, while patriotic hackers appear to suffer no sanction for their brazen contravention of Chinese law. Other analysts begin from the specious premise that since the Chinese government "owns" the Internet in China, patriotic hackers therefore must work for the state. Still others correctly point to the fact that a number of these groups, such as Xfocus and NSFocus, appear to be morphing into "white-hat" hackers (i.e., becoming professional information security professionals), often developing relationships with companies associated with the Ministry of Public Security, or the ministry itself. Yet the evidence suggests that the groups truly are independent actors, more correctly labeled "state tolerated" or "state encouraged." They are tolerated because they are "useful idiots" for the regime, but they are also careful not to pursue domestic hacking activities that might threaten "internal stability" and thereby activate the repression apparatus. Indeed, most of the groups have issued constitutions or other organizing documents that specifically prohibit members from attacking Chinese Web sites or networks.

Even if it is true that patriotic hacker groups are not controlled by the state, Beijing is still worried about the possible effect of their behavior in a crisis with the United States and/or Taiwan. Analysis of several recent "hacker wars" over the past two years suggests an evolving mechanism for shaping the activities of "patriotic hackers." In August 1999, after the conclusion of the cross-Strait hacker skirmish that erupted in the wake of Taiwan President Lee Teng-hui's declaration that the island's relationship to the mainland was a "state-to-state relationship," a *Liberation Army Daily* article lauded the "patriotic hackers" and encouraged other hackers to join in during the next crisis with Taiwan. In April 2001, *Guangzhou Daily* reprinted without attribution a *Wired* article on the impending outbreak of a "hacker war" between Chinese and American hackers, which many hackers saw as a sign of government backing. A media-generated hacker war thereafter ensued, with Chinese and American hackers defacing hundreds, if not thousands, of Web sites. In May 2001, however, an authoritative *People's Daily* article rebuked both Western and Chinese hackers, calling activities by both sides "illegal." This signaled to the hackers that the state had withdrawn its sanction of their activities, and hacker activity quickly tapered off in response to the warning.

A year later, patriotic hacker chat rooms were filled with discussion and planning for a "first anniversary" hacker war. In late April 2002, on the eve of the proposed conflict, *People's Daily* published another unsigned editorial on the subject, decrying the loose talk about a hacker war and warning of serious consequences. Participants in the hacker chat rooms quickly recognized the signal, and the plans for a new hacker war were abandoned. In neither case could this dynamic be called control, but instead they both reflect the population's keen sensitivity to the subtle messages in government propaganda, which continues to successfully create a Leninist climate of self-deterrence and self-censorship that is more powerful than active state repression. As some groups move into "white-hat" positions, however, the relationship might actually transition from a ruler-ruled dynamic to a partnership motivated by reasons ranging from nationalism to naked self-interest.

A final issue related to measuring capability involves the assessment of a group or country's ability to generate new attack tools or exploits. Outside analysts, many of whom are programmers themselves, tend to reify countries like Russia that abound with highly talented programmers, and look down on countries or individuals that simply use off-the-shelf "script kiddie" tools like distributed denial of service (DDOS) programs. DDOS is admittedly a blunt instrument, but a fixation on finding more sophisticated attacks, which reflects the widely held but logically tenuous assumption that state-sponsorship correlates with sophistication, may be counterproductive. Instead, analysts should employ a simple "means-ends" test. In the Chinese case, DDOS, despite its relatively simplicity, looks like the right tool for the right mission. From the Chinese point of view, for example, hammering the NIPRNET and forcing it to be taken down for repairs would be considered an operational success, since it could potentially delay or degrade U.S. logistics deployments to Taiwan.

In conclusion, therefore, a strategy to disrupt U.S. logistics systems with CNA seems well-matched to U.S. vulnerabilities and Chinese capabilities, although the final operational impact of the effort may be undermined by important Chinese misperceptions about political will and the nature of U.S. logistics operations.

Option Three: Missile-Centric Strategies

A possible strategy that China might pursue to counter U.S. military transformation would be a missile-centric one that seeks to present an overwhelming short-range missile threat to Taiwan, improve China's offensive capabilities against U.S. bases in the Asia-Pacific, and give the PLA the capability to launch conventional strikes against U.S. strategic targets. Such an approach would be based on the calculation that enhanced missile capabilities would allow Beijing to increase its leverage over Taiwan and that U.S. apprehension about escalation might deter U.S. military intervention in defense of Taiwan, or at least limit U.S. intervention by discouraging the United States from launching attacks on China itself in such a crisis. As part of this missile-centric force scenario, we consider not only further improvements in China's SRBM arsenal, but also several more speculative possibilities, such as future developments in strategy and force structure that might give China the capability to wage theater and strategic conventional warfare against U.S. targets in Guam, Hawaii, or CONUS with conventionally armed ballistic and cruise missiles. These "high-end" capabilities would be focused against a small set of high-leverage targets that would influence both the political and military underpinnings of operations against China, consistent with relatively modest numbers of delivery systems.[1]

---

[1] Gill, Mulvenon, and Stokes analyze Chinese missile forces at three levels: conventional SRBMs that would be used primarily against Taiwan, theater missiles that could strike targets throughout East Asia, and ICBMs capable of striking targets within the continental

Background

This section explains why a missile-centric force might be plausible. It reviews the background on historical and more recent missile-related developments. It also describes three potential missile-centric strategies, supporting concepts of operations, and force structure combinations: (1) SRBM-centric, (2) regional power projection (i.e., access denial), and (3) limited strategic conventional force (i.e., countervailing conventional forces to deny U.S. ability to wage strategic conventional war).

Chinese Military Modernization and the Missile-Centric Scenario

Chinese military modernization is clearly focused on preparing for a potential Taiwan conflict and U.S. military intervention. Greater military capabilities provide China a greater ability to deter Taiwan from seeking unilateral changes in the status quo and increased political leverage to press for resolution on China's terms, as well as credible options to use force against Taiwan and limit U.S. intervention in the event of a conflict in the Taiwan Strait. DoD assesses that Beijing's main objective in the event of a conflict would be to "compel a quick negotiated solution on terms favorable to Beijing," preferably before the United States can intervene in force.[2] In response to U.S. intervention, China would attempt to weaken the resolve of the United States "by demonstrating the capability to hold at risk—or actually striking—high-value assets."[3] Beijing would seek to contain escalation and keep the geographic scope of the conflict limited.[4]

On balance, it would appear that a missile-centric approach would be consistent with these objectives and with the PLA's capabilities. However, before delving into the implications of a missile-

---

United States. See Bates Gill, James Mulvenon, and Mark Stokes, "The Chinese Second Artillery Corps: Transition to Credible Deterrence," in James C. Mulvenon and Andrew N.D. Yang, eds., *The People's Liberation Army as Organization: Reference Volume v1.0*, Santa Monica, Calif.: RAND Corporation, CF-182-NSRD, 2002.

[2] U.S. Department of Defense (2003).

[3] U.S. Department of Defense (2003), p. 46.

[4] U.S. Department of Defense (2003).

centric force structure for conventional conflict, we need to briefly examine the role of missile forces in their nuclear deterrent role, China's conventional missile doctrine, and the modernization of the Second Artillery's nuclear and conventional forces.

China's Nuclear Strategy

In the view of a prominent Chinese scholar and expert, Chinese nuclear forces and strategy have gone through three stages of development.[5] In the first stage of development, China relied on "existential deterrence" (*cunzaixing weishe*). Although it had a nuclear weapons capability, China lacked delivery systems and had no real means of retaliation. In the second stage, China's strategy was one of "minimal deterrence" (*zuidi weishe*) based on a small but indefinite number of nuclear weapons. Any country that was contemplating launching a nuclear first strike against China would have had to worry about the possibility that at least a few of China's weapons would survive the attack, allowing China to retaliate. It was this uncertainty that China relied on to deter its superpower adversaries from launching a first strike. Minimal deterrence also rested on the premise that a handful of nuclear weapons were sufficient to inflict "unacceptable damage" (*buke renshou de sunshi*) on an adversary, especially if that adversary had only peripheral interests at stake in a conflict. (Chinese strategists note that this fell well short of the McNamara-era Pentagon standards of holding at risk a substantial portion of an adversary's population and industrial capacity even after suffering a preemptive attack.) In the third, current stage of the development of Chinese nuclear forces, China's strategy is one of "credible minimal deterrence" (*zuidi kexin weishe*). Although still based in part on the uncertainty surrounding an indefinite number of nuclear weapons, this strategy relies primarily on highly survivable mobile missiles to ensure that an adversary could not be confident of its ability to locate and strike all of China's nuclear deterrent forces,

---

[5] This paragraph draws on Li Bin, "Nuclear Weapons and International Relations" (核武器与国际关系), briefing presented at the Beijing Student Doctoral Student Union Academic Lecture Series, Beijing University, November 25, 2003.

even if it expended a number of its nuclear weapons. The adversary is thus deterred from launching a first strike because of concerns that China would retaliate with its surviving mobile missiles.

The efficacy of threatening to launch a comprehensive counter-value attack after a counterforce attack has always been somewhat questionable given the ability of the adversary to inflict grievous damage in return. The problem is especially acute for smaller nuclear powers facing a large nuclear power like the United States.[6] Nevertheless, Chinese strategists generally agree that China's nuclear weapons deter other countries from using or threatening to use their nuclear weapons against China. They also view China's possession of nuclear weapons as insurance that the United States cannot treat China like a larger version of Iraq or Serbia. China's status as a nuclear power means the United States must proceed with considerable caution in the event of a military conflict.

Chinese analysts hold a broad range of views on the extent to which nuclear weapons are useful in deterring various types of conventional attacks, however, with some arguing that China should modify or withdraw its "no first use" policy to enhance the utility of nuclear weapons in deterring conventional attacks that would threaten vital national interests. For these advocates, the no-first-use policy is viewed as a real constraint in many Chinese military writings on Second Artillery doctrine, which emphasize that China must rely on dispersal and mobility to maintain a nuclear force that is capable of surviving an enemy nuclear first strike and retaliating in a harsh poststrike environment.[7]

Some Chinese strategists have advocated the development of limited nuclear warfighting capabilities.[8] The majority of available

---

[6] This sort of balance suggests that a controlled retaliatory response is of great interest in the event of deterrence failing.

[7] See, for example, Wang and Zhang (2000), p. 370.

[8] See Alastair Iain Johnston, "Prospects for Chinese Nuclear Force Modernization: Limited Deterrence Versus Multilateral Arms Control," *China Quarterly*, No. 146, June 1996, pp. 548–576, and Alastair Iain Johnston, "China's New 'Old Thinking': The Concept of Limited Deterrence," *International Security*, Vol. 20, No. 3, Winter 1995/1996.

evidence suggests, however, that the modernization of China's strategic nuclear forces is intended primarily to improve the country's survivability, thus enhancing the credibility of China's nuclear deterrent. In short, Beijing's goal is to enhance the credibility of China's strategic deterrence and ensure that it remains credible in the face of U.S. advances in conventional long-range precision strike capabilities and the deployment of missile defense systems.[9]

Chinese strategists are particularly concerned that U.S. deployment of a national missile defense system would undermine China's nuclear retaliatory capability, especially following either a conventional or nuclear attack on their nuclear forces. They worry that this would leave the United States free to challenge vital Chinese interests without fear of nuclear retaliation. In the view of one prominent Chinese strategist, U.S. policy toward China would become "even more unreasonable," as the United States would feel less constrained when considering actions that would harm Chinese national security interests. Although China would proceed with the modernization of its nuclear forces even if the United States elected not to deploy a missile defense system, it would act to protect the effectiveness of its nuclear deterrent in a missile defense environment by deploying penetration aids and missile defense countermeasures, increasing the number of ICBMs, and perhaps deploying missiles with multiple warheads (*duo dantou*).[10]

China's Conventional Missile Doctrine

The Second Artillery was a nuclear retaliation force throughout much of its history. It was not until the end of the Cold War that its mission expanded to include conventional missile operations, and it was only in the mid- to late 1990s that it began to develop a doctrine for

---

[9] See Michael Chase and Evan Medeiros, "China's Evolving Nuclear Calculus: Modernization and the Doctrinal Debate," paper presented at RAND/CNAC PLA conference, Washington, D.C., December 2002.

[10] See Li Bin (2003).

conventional missile attack campaigns.[11] Conventional missile operations have since come to be viewed as the type of operations the Second Artillery is most likely to conduct and as a key component of future PLA campaigns.

Chinese military doctrinal writings indicate that conventional missiles would be used to strike important strategic and campaign-level targets and to support ground, air, and naval operations.[12] This general guidance amounts to hitting what is important and not wasting missiles on the unimportant. Little can be directly inferred from what is said at such a level of generality, except that there is a focus on militarily relevant targets and not against population targets per se. That does not mean that attacks with conventional missiles would necessarily spare civilian infrastructure, but it does suggest that the attacks would be focused to fit into a clear plan that is seeking fairly specific effects.

The PLA does not view its conventional missiles as "silver bullets" that are capable of deciding conflicts and achieving operational and political objectives on their own in the manner advanced by some advocates of aerospace power in the West. Although Chinese strategists point out that conventional missile attack campaigns might be conducted independently under certain circumstances, their writings place much greater emphasis on the importance of the missile forces coordinating with the other services in joint campaigns involving missile, naval, air, and ground forces.[13]

The tight coupling of conventional missiles with theater war plans is consistent with a fairly conservative assessment of both effectiveness of bombardment systems and the appropriateness of such attacks within the universe of potential military operations. This seems typical of the kind of view normally associated with a ground force–centric military. However, experience with Western countries

---

[11] See Ken Allen and Maryanne Kivlehan, "Implementing PLA Second Artillery Doctrinal Reforms," paper presented at the RAND/CNAC PLA conference, Washington, D.C., December 2002.

[12] See, for example, Wang and Zhang (2000).

[13] See, for example, Wang and Zhang (2000).

and the former Soviet Union suggests that as capabilities for reliable precision attacks grow, we will see the development of a new line of thought emphasizing the importance of independent operations.

Possible roles for shorter-range conventional missile operations include deterrence, large-scale missile attacks, missile support to blockades and landing campaigns, and coercive or psychological attacks. In the context of long-range operations throughout the full strategic depth of an adversary, attacks would primarily be directed at damaging vulnerable critical nodes, forcing the adversary to modify behaviors to mitigate damage, and altering the fundamental calculus of the conflict. Each of these roles demands a different operational and technical emphasis for the missile forces. How and to what extent these roles are emphasized are determined by the military and technical capabilities of Chinese missile forces and, perhaps most importantly, by the preferences of commanders for use of the missile forces in such operations.

The Second Artillery's conventional missile forces are expected to play a leading role in deterring Taiwan from undertaking any potentially provocative moves toward independence and limiting the U.S. response should China decide to use force against Taiwan.[14] In this role, the missile forces are the primary rapid strike capability of the PLA. The nature of the attack by the missile force would be adjusted to fit into either a strictly coercive set of attacks designed to influence both popular and elite behavior or against critical force elements in a militarily significant type of operation designed to facilitate broader military operations. While not strictly independent (attacks in either domain could produce effects in the other), the differences in emphasis would be seen in the breadth and depth of attacks against the Taiwanese target system.

---

[14] According to one internal Chinese military source, "when separatist forces attempt to split the country, foreign powers attempt to use military force to intervene in our internal affairs, or our key strategic targets are seriously threatened by the enemy's high-tech weapons, the conventional missile campaign corps of the Second Artillery can conduct missile deterrence combat to contain and foil enemy strategic intentions" (Wang and Zhang, 2000).

Chinese military writings characterize conventional missiles as the most useful weapons in the PLA's inventory for precision deep strike attacks against key enemy targets such as air bases, naval facilities, command and control systems, and early warning and air defense assets. The relative ease of achieving surprise with SRBM strikes is also seen as a major advantage of conventional missile campaigns. These military advantages are combined with the greater ease of use of missiles relative to conventional aircraft, making missile forces especially attractive for operations not requiring repeated and extensive large-scale re-attacks.[15]

In the strategic conventional conflict context, there has not been any evidence of interest in pursuing extremely long-range strike. However, a strategic conventional strike capability, albeit limited, might still be attractive to the Chinese to fill the gap between conventional theater operations and the deterrent mission for their nuclear forces. Conventional strategic strike would decrease the pressure they might experience for launching a limited nuclear option in retaliation for a comprehensive, or even targeted but extremely damaging, U.S. conventional strategic attack on China. Also, there would be possible benefits from accentuating the risks of conventional operations against the Chinese mainland.[16]

Modernization of Chinese Missile Forces

The ongoing modernization of China's missile forces has featured increases in quantity and improvements in quality. Along with rising numbers, there has been a pronounced shift in emphasis toward conventional missile forces and missions. China is also pursuing greater accuracy, shifting from liquid fuel to solid fuel, and moving from fixed launch sites to mobile missiles.

---

[15] Because missile forces are built on expendable, yet still costly, flight elements, very large attacks (weapons numbering in the thousands) tend to be viewed as prohibitively expensive, and there is significant delay in terms of force recapitalization because of the cost and time needed to produce replacement missile airframes.

[16] The threat of nuclear escalation is less plausible the lower the level of violence, so China's nuclear forces may not be adequate to deter lesser attacks on China.

Nuclear Force Modernization: Enhancing Survivability and Ensuring Sufficiency. China currently has about 20 CSS-4 ICBMs. The CSS-4s are large, liquid propellant, silo-based missiles armed with single nuclear warheads. China has the capability to develop and deploy a multiple reentry vehicle system for its CSS-4 ICBMs, according to the unclassified summary of the 2002 National Intelligence Estimate on foreign missile developments.[17] The Second Artillery also fields about a dozen CSS-3 ICBMs, which are capable of striking targets in Asia, and a medium-range submarine-launched ballistic missile (SLBM). According to the same source, the intelligence community projects that, by 2015, China will have 75 to 100 warheads deployed on its strategic missiles, as well as about two dozen shorter range DF-31 and CSS-3 ICBMs capable of reaching parts of the United States.[18] Most of these missiles will be mobile. The solid propellant mobile missiles that will enter the force during that time period (the DF-31 and DF-31A follow-on ICBMs and the JL-2 SLBM) constitute the cornerstones of China's effort to develop and deploy a "modern, mobile, and more survivable strategic missile force."[19]

The key element for the Chinese strategic forces is the development of survivable strategic missiles as the necessary, but not sufficient, condition for having an assured retaliatory force. The development of the DF-31 family of missiles is extremely important in that it gives the Chinese the *option* of operating their forces in a survivable basing mode. The development of the DF-31 family *does not* assure that the forces will in fact be survivable, or controllable, should they be deployed away from their main operating bases (MOBs). The mobility of the DF-31 family of missiles allows for its movement away from easily targeted locations, but unless great effort is made to support and operate the missiles for extended periods away from

---

[17] U.S. National Intelligence Council, *Foreign Missile Developments and the Ballistic Missile Threat Through 2015: Unclassified Summary of a National Intelligence Estimate*, 2001.

[18] U.S. National Intelligence Council (2001).

[19] U.S. National Intelligence Council (2001).

MOBs, they will not really be able to be counted as survivable should a protracted military campaign take place.[20]

In addition to the modernization of the more survivable portion of its deterrent force, China is also replacing its aging fleet of CSS-4 Mod 1 ICBMs with CSS-4 Mod 2 missiles. [21] The primary benefits of the new missiles are enhanced accuracy and a platform capable (by virtue of its throw-weight and large payload volume) of relatively simple adaptation of MIRVs (multiple independently targetable re-entry vehicles) or other advanced reentry and decoy systems. There is also the possibility of using such missiles to carry specialized nuclear warheads such as high-yield nuclear weapons to produce EMP.

While the United States, Great Britain, and France have invested heavily in their SSBN (nuclear-powered fleet ballistic missile submarine) forces to provide robust retaliatory capabilities, China seems to be pursuing a more modest program that will field only small number of moderate capability SLBMs. The Chinese SLBM force will include JL-1 SLBMs on Xia SSBNs and JL-2s on Type 094 SSBNs.[22] Such a modest force could provide an assured retaliatory capability only if deployed to sea in a way in which it would have reasonable expectation of eluding detection and avoiding destruction by attack submarines or other antiship warfare forces. The operation of small SSBN forces, depending on the level of confidence required in that force, could prove to be a fairly difficult proposition in the face of a large and well-trained adversary. In the game of offense and defense, the concern by the SSBN operator is that the unexpected

---

[20] Mobile missiles are subject to a host of possible attacks both in transit and in their concealed deployment locations. The longer they are in the field at war reserve locations, the greater their chance of discovery and possible destruction by conventional or nuclear attack. While the attacker may not be confident of their ability to neutralize Chinese mobile missiles, a conservative PLA planner may not likewise be confident in survival of their systems absent significant numbers of missiles and fairly robust basing means.

[21] U.S. Department of Defense (2003), p. 31.

[22] U.S. Department of Defense (2003), p. 31.

deployment of defenders to a key sea region might catastrophically affect a small SSBN force.[23]

Conventional Missile Force Modernization. China has deployed about 450 SRBMs, and the PLA is expected to add about 75 more missiles to its inventory in each of the next few years. According to the unclassified version of the annual report to the U.S. Congress on China's military power, China is increasing the accuracy and lethality of its SRBMs and developing modified versions of the CSS-6 that could employ satellite-aided navigation and are capable of striking U.S. forces in Okinawa as well as numerous targets on Taiwan. China is also developing land-attack cruise missiles and a conventional version of the CSS-5 medium-range ballistic missile.[24]

Three Potential Missile-Centric Strategies

There are three major variants in the makeup of a future missile-centric force. The variants are identified based on the area of impact desired for the force: a short-range force characterized by predominance of SRBM systems, a regional force characterized by the added ability to hold at risk targets out to the range of Guam, and finally a true strategic force that adds the ability to hold at risk some set of targets in CONUS.

SRBM-Centric. The SRBM-centric force is characterized by the extensive deployment of SRBMs intended to cover targets along the near periphery of China. Such a force could hold at risk fixed, relocatable, and select mobile targets. The most important aspect of this force is that it is focused almost exclusively on operations near the Chinese homeland and would be focused almost exclusively on their regional foes and on combat forces of allies (e.g., U.S. forces) moving into the theater. The missile forces could have a central role in a variety of campaigns, ranging from coercion campaigns to supporting broader military operations.

---

[23] The defender cannot count on getting those lucky breaks, but neither can prudent Chinese commanders discount the possibility of such an outcome.

[24] U.S. Department of Defense (2003), p. 29.

A consequence of concentrating on shorter-range forces is the acceptance that sanctuary bases might exist outside the range of the missile force. As a result, other combat elements would have to deal with American forces at these bases, *or* China would have to accept some significant damage from U.S. combat forces operating from de facto sanctuary locations.

Regional Power Projection. Another option would be a regional power projection force designed to hold at risk U.S. forces operating out of bases in Japan, South Korea, the Philippines, and Guam. This option builds on the SRBM-centric force's ability to inflict damage along the periphery and removes the de facto sanctuary status of U.S. bases throughout the region. The regional missile-centric option is very interesting for the Chinese because of the tendency of U.S. planners not to implement the measures necessary to ensure the operation of bases as well as the intrinsic problem of sheltering large aircraft necessary to operate from distant locations. This option is especially interesting from a geopolitical perspective, since it opens up options against U.S. allies, in both the prewar period and wartime, that might result in reducing U.S. operations in the region.

Limited Strategic Conventional Force. The third possibility is a limited strategic conventional force designed to provide China with conventional strike options for use against targets in Hawaii, Alaska, and perhaps even CONUS. The principal goal of such a limited strategic conventional force would be to deny the United States the ability to wage strategic conventional war against China with impunity. It would give the PLA a capability that it presently lacks: the option of launching conventional strikes against military targets in CONUS in retaliation for U.S. attacks against strategic targets in China. Should China and the United States come into conflict over Taiwan, this capability might allow Chinese leaders to demonstrate to their political rivals and to the Chinese public that China is retaliating in kind for U.S. strikes against the mainland. Furthermore, a carefully crafted attack could have a significant impact on U.S. military operations either through destruction of key assets or more likely forcing U.S. planners to honor the threat and to change how operations are conducted.

Rationale

A missile-centric option is very attractive to the Chinese for many reasons. The major rationales fall into three broad categories: those based on matching the military and technical strengths of the Chinese, those based on exploiting some apparent weaknesses in U.S. military plans for direct military effect, and those based on altering the political environment by being able to hold at risk a small subset of targets capable of producing maximum political effect.

Matching Chinese Military and Technical Capabilities

Missile forces represent a good match for the military and technical capabilities of the PLA. In terms of operational complexity, missile operations tend to be much less demanding than many other types of conventional force operations. Mission planning can be readily accomplished from centralized locations, and execution of attacks typically requires less on-the-fly adaptation than air operations. Given the PLA's limited, though improving, training and expertise, this would seem to be a way of addressing weaknesses in the ability of its forces to execute more complex operations.

In terms of technology, missile forces are a similarly good match with PLA and defense industry capabilities. Missile forces can be relatively simple in design and still retain much of their effectiveness. In part this is due to the offense-defense balance that has generally favored the offense for an extended period. This can be contrasted with manned air operations, which have driven manned aircraft and defense systems such as Patriot and the SA-20 to more and more complex and expensive designs. Missiles, however, have presented a more difficult problem for the defense and have the advantage of attack strategies exploiting saturation, leakage, and exhaustion to defeat defenders. This means that fairly old designs from a Western perspective (say on the order of 30 years old) retain significant advantages in some situations.

The intrinsic simplicity of combat missile operations allows the most difficult part of the force employment problem to be transferred from those who employ the systems in the field to those who design and build the systems. This basic approach, which avoids complexity at the field level, is a well-established way of dealing with the limited expertise of the bulk of the troops and keeps operations and maintenance costs as low as possible.[25]

Another rationale for the missile force is that the other options for power projection—air and naval forces—are both very difficult and costly to develop if the focus for that force is the United States. The United States possesses arguably the only significant "blue-water navy" and the single most powerful Air Force in the world. The use of network-centric techniques and the development of advanced munitions have further increased the capability of these two force elements. Attempting a head-on challenge would necessitate development of a large and highly capable force, which would prove daunting for any nation. However, development of systems based on expendables, particularly systems that are difficult to counter such as ballistic missiles, would appear attractive if the total size of the target system to be attacked were small.[26]

Exploiting Weaknesses

A related issue that makes missile forces attractive is an increasing tendency on the part of U.S. planners to focus on a smaller number of high-capability systems and bases for operations, all the while exploiting networking to increase the combat capability of their numerically smaller force.[27] This small number of targets, as well as

---

[25] For the United States, the use of "wooden rounds" requiring less maintenance by field personnel has been regarded as a great success and seems to be a general trend in regard to many combat systems. In part, this is traceable to the use of storable consumables (fuels, lubricants, etc.) and the advent of wide-scale use of environmental canisters for storage and transport.

[26] Ballistic missiles are relatively costly on a per-target basis because of the significant airframe cost and non-reusability of the airframe. However, as long as the target system is constrained, the avoidance of huge fixed costs associated with the development of complex platforms (ships and planes) along with the high probability of penetrating defenses make them attractive for some missions. The interesting question for the PLA is where the crossover point is for the costly expendable missile systems currently being pursued.

[27] The MC2A aircraft program exemplifies this tendency in which the functionality of several aircraft is being combined on a smaller number of more capable systems. The use of

the time needed for replacement platforms and key elements such as sensor suites, means the U.S. advantage may be sufficiently diminished for an extended enough period to alter the way in which the United States conducts military operations.[28] Also, but perhaps most importantly in terms of pervasive effects, the ability to hold at risk targets can create an effect likened to virtual attrition. Here the U.S. planners are forced to "honor" the threat and take appropriate action to lessen their vulnerability to attack. Such mitigation measures might dramatically decrease the willingness to concentrate key assets at vulnerable locations, force the dedication of scarce ISR and analytic resources to locating and tracking threats, and perhaps force different investment strategies than otherwise might be pursued in a more benign environment. Indeed, the ability to hold at risk some key targets on installations throughout the full strategic depth might be a very interesting capability to Chinese military planners interested both in decreasing the willingness of the United States to attack targets in China and in altering U.S. behavior.

Theater missile forces are the key to the warfighting capability of a missile force. Here, weapons would be deigned to confront both Taiwanese and U.S. military planners with a difficult problem. The vast majority of U.S. capability to strike at the enemy and, more importantly from the standpoint of keeping Taiwan in the fight, defend against enemy attack unfortunately is constrained by relatively short-legged aircraft. These platforms are dependent on either fixed bases or aircraft carriers that need to approach the immediate battle zone. In both cases, missile forces offer the possibility of brief "closeout" capabilities (excluding operations for limited periods of time) and even lessening the U.S. willingness to conduct routine opera-

---

UAVs is countering this trend to a limited degree, but the United States has shown a general preference for smaller number of high-capability systems such as Global Hawk in part because of the desire to use high-quality (and costly) sensor suites to deal with very difficult problems.

[28] It is not clear whether having the United States change would always be advantageous for China. The possibility exists for the United States to employ brute-force techniques to many of these problems, and until that capability is vitiated, the possibility of changing the conflict to a less desirable form always needs to remain in the mind of Chinese planners.

tions. If these periods can be synchronized with other operations designed to win the battle to influence both public and elite perceptions of the problem, such operations would have a significant strategic impact.

In a more narrow military sense, theater missiles would also be useful in decreasing the ability of the U.S. and Taiwanese militaries to conduct effective operations. Attacks on unhardened airfields could either shut down or dramatically decrease the sortie generation capability of the attacked airfields. Attacks would be directed against unsheltered aircraft, soft infrastructure such as aboveground fueling, critical support facilities, and operations centers. The resultant decrease in U.S. and Taiwan sortie rates would augment the ability of China to conduct conventional military operations (particularly air strikes using manned aircraft) or perhaps even improve the ability of invasion forces moving across the Strait. Whether such attacks would be successful would largely depend on the ability of the bases to generate sufficient sorties while under attack or the availability of alternate locations.[29]

The issue of operating locations is a very important one, since key U.S. bases are dependent on host governments agreeing to both their presence and their use in operations against China. Here the Chinese might take advantage of a number of factors that could influence the host government to drastically restrict or eliminate the possibility of operations being conducted from their territory. Missile forces offer an interesting capability that might be able to hold at risk not only military facilities but other value structure targets to increase the perceived cost of allowing U.S. intervention in what China would argue is an internal Chinese matter. At the very least, having a sufficient missile force to deny the United States use of its primary and secondary bases would be an advantage, particularly if the secondary bases have large unhardened infrastructure that might serve as attractive targets.

---

[29] The United States planned to operate airfields in Europe under heavy conventional air attack. To sustain operations, it deployed active defenses, built hardened shelters, dispersed key force elements, and planned for rapid repairs and reconstitution of facilities.

Chinese commentators appear to believe that the threat of missile attack would drive a wedge between the United States and its principal allies in the region, especially Japan. Specifically, China probably calculates that missile threats would diminish Japanese willingness to allow unrestricted use of U.S. military bases in a Taiwan scenario. Chinese writings on military strategy emphasize the importance of exploiting potential fissures in alliance relationships, and some Chinese military officers have suggested in published articles that Japan would become a legitimate target for Chinese missile attack if it allowed the United States to operate from bases on its territory in a Taiwan conflict. Chinese military officers have also told Western scholars that Beijing would try to coerce Tokyo into refusing to allow U.S. forces to use Japanese bases in a Taiwan conflict. In the words of one PLA officer, "we shall tell Japan that if they allow the United States to use bases there [in the conflict], we shall have to strike them!"[30]

As to whether missile forces offer the real opportunity for compellence, the issue is far from clear. Selective attacks against key targets are all that is possible with a force numbering only in the hundreds of accurate weapons. U.S. experience with precision air attacks has been mixed in terms of its ability to affect both popular and elite decisionmaking. If the issue is not central to the parties, limited amounts of force can help the targeted group see that acquiescence is in its rational self-interest. Another effect, delaying of decisions, can be more readily expected as the on-the-spot decisionmaker hesitates to grant permission while a consensus is built. Such delay might be very useful tactically, although the strategic impact of simply delaying operations is not readily apparent.

However, attacks can have the unintentional effect of increasing the resolve of the targeted population. The possibility of strengthened resolve in the face of attack is difficult to ignore, even if some short-term gain is realized from hesitation at the start of operations. The uncertainty associated with compellence operations against host

---

[30] See David Shambaugh, *Modernizing China's Military: Progress, Problems, and Prospects,* Berkeley, Calif.: University of California Press, 2002, p. 309.

countries suggest that while they might be a part of the campaign, they cannot be counted on to produce the desired military impact. This suggests that their primary function in the context of these host countries is to shape the political environment, particularly prior basing arrangements (granting of standing basing rights, default approval of operations, etc.), as well as forcing U.S. planners to consider the possibility of such attacks.

The potential addition of long-range conventional systems capable of striking regional bases such as Guam, or deep bases in Hawaii or CONUS, offer yet another set of capabilities to military planners in China. While the use of such capabilities would entail significant risk of a wider conflict, their presence gives options to both the military and political leadership to respond to attacks against vital interests inside China without resorting to the use of nuclear weapons.

Altering Political Calculations

Perhaps most importantly, China may calculate that in a conflict over Taiwan, the asymmetry of interests between China and the United States would allow China to use its missile forces to deny the United States escalation dominance. Beijing would have much more at stake than Washington in the event of a showdown over the status of Taiwan. For Washington, Taiwan's security is undoubtedly an important U.S. interest, as reflected by the Taiwan Relations Act and subsequent statements and actions emphasizing the United States' commitment to the island's defense. For Beijing, however, Taiwan ranks as the most important security issue, and Chinese leaders have stated their willingness to "pay any price" to resolve the issue on terms favorable to Beijing, or at least to prevent a change in the status quo that they would view as an unacceptable affront to Chinese interests. In a conflict over Taiwan, Beijing calculates that China's vital national interests, and perhaps even regime survival, would be on the line. Chinese leaders perceive this asymmetry of the interests at stake as a factor that would make Chinese threats to escalate more credible than U.S. threats as well as a potential source of leverage in a crisis or conflict.

Chinese officials have made a number of statements intended to underscore their view that the balance of interests favors China. The best-known comment is probably General Xiong Guangkai's infamous remark to former U.S. Assistant Secretary of Defense Ambassador Chas Freeman. "In the 1950s," Xiong reportedly said, "you three times threatened nuclear strikes on China, and you could do that because we couldn't hit back. Now we can. So you are not going to threaten us again because, in the end, you care a lot more about Los Angeles than Taipei."[31] Though frequently misinterpreted as a specific nuclear threat against Los Angeles, the remark was more likely intended to convey two related messages: that China's possession of nuclear weapons would prevent the United States from using threats of nuclear escalation to compel China to back down in a future Taiwan crisis, and that Beijing is willing to pay a higher price than Washington is in a conflict over Taiwan because the outcome would be more important to China than to the United States.

More recently, Chinese Premier Wen Jiabao warned in a November 2003 interview that China would "pay any price" to prevent Taiwan's permanent separation from the mainland.[32] Later that month, senior military officers assigned to China's Academy of Military Sciences expanded on Wen's comments, declaring China's willingness to accept the loss of the 2008 Olympics, declining foreign investment, damage to China's foreign relations, temporary disruption of the Chinese economy, and heavy military and civilian casualties as the necessary consequences of using force against Taiwan to prevent the island's formal independence.[33]

---

[31] See Barton Gellman, "U.S. and China Nearly Came to Blows in '96; Tension Over Taiwan Prompted Repair of Ties," *Washington Post*, June 21, 1998.

[32] John Pomfret and Philip P. Pan, "Chinese Premier Presses U.S. on Taiwan, Trade," *Washington Post*, November 23, 2003.

[33] Joseph Kahn, "Chinese Officers Say Taiwan's Leaders Are Near 'Abyss of War'," *New York Times*, December 4, 2003b. See also "Military Experts Discuss War to Oppose 'Taiwan Independence'" (军事专家谈反台独战争), *People's Daily Online*, November 27, 2003. This article reprints the comments of the military officers from a previous article published in *Liaowang* [Outlook], the weekly magazine of the official Xinhua news agency. To further reinforce this message, the official *People's Daily* subsequently reprinted Wen's comments

In addition to accentuating and capitalizing on the asymmetry of interests, the very presence of such nonnuclear strategic weapons would alter the dynamics in a way that could prove useful to the Chinese. Even if the weapons were never employed, their presence would compel a prudent commander to consider their possible employment and ways of mitigating attacks by protecting vulnerable assets. Such defensive actions might consist of passive measures such as hardening targets, alterations of deployment plans to preferentially move theater defenses into place, and shifts in investments to provide defenses against missiles at the expense of militarily useful systems. The end result might be that the United States deploys a slower and less offensively capable force into the region during the early days of a campaign, hoping to terminate the conflict prior to a major U.S. force arriving in theater.

If the United States chooses to attack the Chinese conventional strategic forces early in a conflict to remove their threat to U.S. forces, such an attack might also be advantageous politically and diplomatically from the Chinese perspective. A large attack capable of destroying the Chinese forces could be portrayed as an effort by the United States to remove a firebreak between conventional and nuclear combat. Although not ideal from a military standpoint, it might make the U.S. position in the conflict less tenable and assist the Chinese in efforts to deny U.S. regional basing options.

If Chinese conventional strategic weapons are actually used, there are several different ways in which they might help China. First, they might directly inflict damage against key targets that would disrupt U.S. operations in the early days of a conflict. Of particular importance would be disruption of critical air, naval, and supporting forces attempting to establish air and naval supremacy in the theater of operations. Second, they might force expenditure of limited national missile defense assets to intercept conventional payloads and

---

and the remarks of the Academy of Military Sciences officers. See "PLA: Chen Shui-bian Is to Blame If War Breaks Out," *People's Daily Online*, December 3, 2003.

decoys. A possible benefit of a conventional strike on CONUS would be to compel the United States to engage the incoming missiles. Since U.S. planners can never be sure of the weapons payload prior to impact, defensive missiles would have to be employed to engage the incoming warheads and nondiscriminated decoys. The end result might be a severe depletion of U.S. missile defenses, bolstering the perceived capability of even a limited nuclear second strike. In this case, the attractiveness of a preemptive option would decrease as the potency of Chinese missiles is enhanced by the degradation of U.S. missile defense capabilities.

Finally, through a combination of direct kinetic effects and altered perceptions as to the nature of the conflict, the conventional strategic forces might alter the political climate in a way compatible with Chinese interests. The alteration of the political climate might be very important to both the Chinese military and political leadership in terms of assisting with any sort of war termination strategy. Once the Chinese and U.S. forces are joined in combat, the only real hope for the Chinese is to convince the U.S. side to break off combat operations. A victory based on compelling the United States to acquiesce would not be possible because of the drastic asymmetry of force available and the possibility of the United States pursuing a long quasi-war strategy to seriously harm central Chinese interests globally. A plausible Chinese approach would emphasize the internal nature of the conflict, as well as the reckless escalation of the United States in both waging conventional local war and escalating the conflict to the strategic level through its attack on "strategic second strike" conventional forces.[34] The assistance of other nations interested in decreasing the risk of nuclear weapons release might be helpful in ending the war on the most favorable terms possible.

---

[34] The success of this kind of strategy is in fact a bit problematic, but once the fateful decision has been made to risk a direct confrontation with the United States, this may be one of the better of a set of low-percentage options for the Chinese leadership.

Feasibility

In evaluating the feasibility of Chinese pursuit of a missile-centric strategy in response to U.S. military transformation, a number of variables, including R&D, production, and operational issues, as well as strategic considerations are reviewed. The feasibility of the missile-centric strategy is based on considerations such as the research and development base to support missile development, production capacity to meet the operational requirements of warfighters, the matching of numbers and characteristics of delivery systems to their target sets, and the likely payoff for such a strategy given the realities of the PLA's ability to produce and operate such a system.

Can It Be Built?

At the most basic level, it appears that China is on the cusp of being able to build a viable missile-centric force structure. China has demonstrated most of the critical technologies to produce operationally useful missiles with sufficient accuracy to hold at risk their primary targets of interest. The incremental development of Chinese missile system–related technologies in the various research centers, along with the concomitant production technologies, sets the stage for larger-scale serial production of warfighting systems possessing a variety of ranges. Of particular importance has been the marriage of accurate guidance and navigation technologies with modern solid-fuel missiles. This combination of accuracy with a reliable and mobile missile force allows for the practical consideration of a missile-centric strategy.[35]

There are some differences worth mentioning with regard to the unique demands of long-range systems versus those of shorter-range systems. The guidance and navigation problems, as well as the propulsion requirements, for intercontinental systems are much more severe than for shorter-range systems. The need for very-high-quality

---

[35] A modern missile is characterized by a high specific impulse propulsion system, with sufficiently smooth burn characteristics and thrust-termination systems to allow the guidance system to steer the missile accurately toward its target.

guidance and navigation systems, even allowing for the update by external reference such as GPS, GLONASS, or Galileo, is still quite demanding. Small errors accumulate over long flights, and the ability to mechanize all the systems is in fact more challenging for long-range systems.

Propulsion technologies are also challenging because they need to be married to a transportable system. Whereas shorter-range systems can have less efficient rocket engines and still stay within militarily manageable weight and size constraints, the mobile long-range systems are vulnerable to small changes in efficiency, leading to significant growth in the size of the missile or falling below critical performance goals in terms of carrying useful payloads at desired ranges.

For nuclear systems, the above factors feed back to designers of the warheads and physics packages. The result is a dance between the missile and payload designers to adapt to the limitations of both elements. The incredibly destructive nature of nuclear warheads allows for a fair degree of flexibility (trading yield and accuracy across a forgiving design range) as long as soft installations are the primary targets, and only a very small number of warheads are needed per missile.

Conventional weapons, however, need to strike in very close proximity to the target and need fairly massive payloads to produce their effects as long as "dumb" munitions are being used. This means that at long ranges an individual missile will be much larger and expensive (because of better guidance and navigation, more energetic propellants, tighter production tolerances, etc.) than their shorter-range counterparts. This means that there is a practical limit to how many of these long-range systems can be procured and the kinds of targets that can be readily addressed by those systems. This point is illustrated when one considers attacks against two notional adversary air bases. In one case, a base has a small parking area for extremely high-value aircraft, uses a small number of soft buildings to maintain and shelter aircraft, and consequently presents an attractive target for a preplanned attack. Another base spreads the aircraft over a very large number of possible parking areas, making a preplanned attack against the installation much more demanding in terms of the number of weapons needed. The former is a good candidate for attack by the long-range conventional missile systems employing simple submunitions, while the latter may not be nearly as attractive a target absent a change in the missile payload to allow a much larger coverage for each missile strike.

Most of the discussion in this chapter has focused on a missile-centric strategy using ballistic missiles as the primary system. In part, this mirrors the strong preference shown by the PLA for these types of missile systems. However, there is the very real possibility that inexpensive cruise missiles would be pursued as level-of-effort weapons (i.e., those employed in sufficient quantity to be employed across the broad spectrum of targets) and could be employed as an integral part of a missile-centric force structure. Such missiles need not follow the path of Western cruise missiles that exploit stealth and exquisite mission planning to accomplish their task. Low-cost long-range cruise missiles, patterned on the Western Joint Direct Attack Munition (JDAM) model of development (very low cost, dependant on external reference system for guidance, insensitive to individual vehicle attrition) can be deployed without imposing undue demands in terms of engineering or production requirements. Such missiles are individually vulnerable, but when employed, especially after defense suppression attacks, could be effective against the dispersed combat forces of nearby nations, as well as dispersed infrastructure targets.[36]

Does It Work?

The big question is whether such a missile-centric force could be effective. The short answer is, it depends. A missile-centric force employing accurate weapons could hold at risk a substantial number of militarily useful targets. Medium-hardened targets are not as much at risk from this class of weapons until they achieve near-precision targeting levels of accuracy better than 10 meters CEP (circular error probable). When accuracies are 3 meters or better, attacks against

---

[36] Systems such as these have been proposed by U.S. defense contractors as a means of allowing conventional signature aircraft to operate outside of long-range surface-to-air missiles and terminal fighter coverage without resorting to higher-cost missiles.

hard-point targets become much more feasible with reasonably sized warheads.

The perceived utility of a missile-centric force is obviously dependent on what is expected of the force in the first place. Holding at risk targets is only the first step of conducting a campaign. What matters is whether those are the right targets and whether the destruction of those targets would produce effects consistent with the Chinese achieving their military and political objectives. A scorecard for the effectiveness of these systems would reflect their ability to strike several hundred soft area targets (such as aircraft in the open) and a few hundred point-soft targets with unitary weapons. Modified missiles equipped with improved guidance systems could also strike at mobile or relocatable high-value targets.

The experience of the United States in conducting large-scale air attacks using weapons like JDAM is such that a capability would be able to cause serious short-term disruption to key infrastructure targets, could cause serious damage to exposed combat force elements (aircraft in the open or other similar targets), and could affect enemy operations in a profound manner. However, such effects on many targets would be transitory, and reconstitution of key elements targeted could be expected to take place rapidly. Capital items, such as planes, could not be readily repaired in the short run, but substitutes from outside the theater could be brought in as replacements over the longer term.

In the military sphere, this suggests that the missile forces would only provide short-term capabilities against an opposing force that holds the majority of its capability outside the theater of operations. Success or failure would not be contingent on this force element but would be dependent on other force elements to compel action prior to reinforcements arriving. Holding at risk the bulk of force in remote locations would not really be feasible given the payload mass required, but holding even a subset at risk could have a disproportionately significant impact on U.S. operations.

However, in the political sphere the story may be much different. Missile forces are ideal as a tool for threatening the infliction of pain. The potential suddenness of the attack, as well as the ability to inflict damage in discrete increments, makes these forces attractive in a coercive campaign. Here the missiles are essentially a kinetic element of an information operation designed to affect the psychology of the opponent. Damage would never be significant enough to defeat an adversary when looked at objectively, but the pain of such attacks, backed even by the remote possibility of combined military operations, might have a significant influence on the decisionmaking of the opponent. For the United States in particular, the removal of sanctuary bases throughout the Pacific theater would be very disconcerting for decisionmakers. The possibility of a symmetric widening of the conflict to conventional strategic war may not prevent force-on-force engagements but may limit the willingness of U.S. decisionmakers to contemplate large-scale attacks into China proper.

Potential Results

In the context of the theater operations, perhaps the greatest impact would be on the ability of U.S. forces to crowd into a small number of bases with the expectation that operations would be feasible and that the aircraft in the theater would not suffer undue attrition while sitting at their bases. Absent empty hardened shelters on bases, aircraft flowing into theater would have to deploy to exposed locations and would have to be dispersed around parking areas at bases as well as perhaps to other locations. Dispersal to remote locations would only be truly helpful if the Chinese lack a sufficient number of deep attack weapons and the requisite ISR to facilitate attack on exposed U.S. forces. If aircraft are to deploy only to hardened shelters, then the number of shelters would cap the maximum number of deployed assets.[37]

---

[37] During the Cold War, the United States and NATO operated a large number of hardened bases both to cope with the size of the problem on the central front and to ensure the availability of an adequate number of air assets even when the bases were attacked or when shut down by Soviet air and missile attacks.

Another impact of the missile-centric force can be seen in how host countries respond to the possible threat of missile attack. In the case of a conflict involving Taiwan, the key nation, aside from Taiwan itself, is Japan. Here the issues are the willingness to allow the United States to operate combat aircraft from bases inside Japan, build additional infrastructure, or allow dispersal of U.S. aircraft (potentially to Japanese bases) for operations. A sufficiently robust capability to threaten attack, as well as adept information operations directed at highlighting the disparity of Japan's interests from those of Taiwan (which would be portrayed as the instigator of any crisis) and the United States (who the Chinese would attempt to portray as a hegemonic power). The deployment of potent Chinese missile forces would likely drive the United States to take corrective actions, such as dispersal and hardening. The Chinese could highlight these preparations in their discussions with the Japanese, possibly causing some sort of pre-conflict crisis over preparation for operations in the event of a China-Taiwan conflict and thus advancing a larger goal of diminishing presence in the region.

Any alteration in flow of forces into the theater and sortie generation capability, prior to the bases being attacked, can be thought of as a sort of virtual attrition of the force. Whether such virtual attrition meets any military objective is another question, but it does in fact make it harder for the United States to intervene with substantial mass in the very early days of a crisis.

Deeper attacks, both in the extended region back to Hawaii and all the way to CONUS, could possibly trigger a number of events both favorable and unfavorable for the Chinese. Reactions to the fielding of any significant Chinese conventional deep-attack capability that could hold at risk some critical U.S. assets would likely be disproportionate to the number of weapons fielded by the Chinese. Moving from what is assumed as a benign environment to one in which attacks might occur throughout the strategic depth requires decisionmakers to contemplate a host of protective measures that would use up scarce resources, force changes in deployment plans and basing that would negatively impact operations, and could delay the commitment of forces during a crisis period until the force is shifted to a survivable posture.

In terms of wartime use, Chinese missile strategies could present U.S. decisionmakers with a dilemma in regard to the use of missile defense assets to counter the attack. If the Chinese launched on the order of 20 or so conventional ICBMs equipped with several reentry vehicles per missile, as well as some countermeasures, a U.S. commander would have to decide whether to allow the missiles to strike the CONUS, exposing the United States to damage, or seriously deplete the ready interceptor force to engage this large number of targets. If they chose the former, there is always a remote chance a nuclear payload would be mixed into the attack package (perhaps a warhead tailored for an EMP attack) or that the conventionally armed missiles would hit one of the relatively unprotected critical locations in the CONUS. However, if they do engage the missiles, then the effectiveness of Chinese nuclear forces, even after a conventional or nuclear preemptive attack, would be greatly enhanced. Given the U.S. statements in regard to preemption, Chinese conventional attacks that alter the balance in favor of the surviving Chinese nuclear forces could be seen as an attempt at stabilizing the situation after attacks deep into China by U.S. forces that might attempt to draw down China's nuclear forces.

Conventional ICBMs might also assist in Chinese war termination efforts. Although the Chinese literature is notable for the absence of serious and detailed discussion of war termination, a prudent Chinese leader would need to consider ways in which both China and U.S. forces could disengage without a fight to the death. Here the conventional ICBMs help primarily by denying the United States the convenient option of waging conventional strategic war against the Chinese without fear of damage and by highlighting that the last step available to the Chinese prior to nuclear weapons usage has been taken. The hope here is that the danger of escalation would be much clearer to the United States and that some sort of cease-fire would be preferable.[38]

There are many undesirable consequences of even limited conventional attacks on the U.S. homeland that might mitigate against China's use of conventional ICBMs in situations other then a response to U.S. attacks on the Chinese mainland. First, the very nature of the ICBM attacks makes it very difficult to reliably distinguish a conventional and nuclear attack until the weapons impact. Unlike the Cold War, there would not be a requirement to launch-out from under the attack, but there would exist the possibility that U.S. leadership might implement alternate command and control procedures that would ensure effective positive control of nuclear forces in the event critical leaderships had been struck with nuclear weapons. The resultant change in both the posture of force elements and command and control could have unfortunate consequences for crisis stability. While these protection efforts would be less serious than those planned for large-scale nuclear attacks, there would be an increased possibility for the unintentional escalation of the conflict.

Second, there is the real danger that the United States might alter its wartime objectives after attacks against its homeland. What started as a limited war focused on Taiwan might shift to the framework of a general war with the United States. This type of shift would expose the Chinese to protracted quasi-war with the United States in which a combination of military, economic, and political action would seek to seriously harm China, or even an intensive "hot war" in which the objective would be to eliminate all Chinese power projection capability, followed by a long Cold War–like period of active containment. In either of these cases, the gain from the attack on CONUS would be more than outweighed by the final losses.

---

[38] This assumes that the Chinese are willing to gamble with approaching the threshold of a more general war to the degree their posture would dissuade the United States from extending the conflict beyond the realm of localized theater operations. If the Chinese and United States have not thought through this issue, any war termination efforts would be ad hoc and more prone to trigger unintended consequences such as a widening of the conflict.

U.S. Responses to Missile-Centric Strategies

In the previous section, we discussed in general terms the interaction of Chinese and U.S. actions. There are a number of specific options that emerge as interesting candidates for further analysis. In this section, we look at a few of these more in depth as a U.S. responses to potential Chinese development and deployment of a much larger and more capable force of strategic, theater, and short-range missiles, including missiles armed with conventional warheads of various types that would be capable of striking targets in theater and in CONUS.

Strategic Actions

Strategic actions in this context refer to sets of activities designed to fundamentally alter the course of the conflict. In regard to Chinese missile forces, this refers to approaches intended to either decrease the likelihood such forces are employed or, if they are employed, decrease their effectiveness by adopting an overall approach to the conflict that minimizes their disruption of U.S. war plans. There are four basic approaches that bound the problem space:

- Self-moderation: Avoid triggering Chinese actions through self-restraint.
- Render irrelevant: Make Chinese actions irrelevant to the successful execution of U.S. war plans.
- Render ineffective: Protect against Chinese missile-centric forces by directly countering the force elements through active and passive means.
- Deterrence: Increase the costs of employing such weapons by adopting a strategy of escalation dominance.

Self-Moderation. Self-moderation can best be thought of as the process of setting boundaries for U.S. war plans in regard to attacking China's homeland. The essence of this approach is to avoid triggering unwanted escalation by refraining from striking the Chinese mainland or at least withholding attacks against important targets on the Chinese mainland, all the while accepting the probability of exposing both U.S. forces and Taiwan to significant missile attack during the opening days of the war. This sort of approach treats escalation (and the concomitant risk of escalation to nuclear weapons use) as an unwanted outcome and adapts U.S. military posture to provide a means of controlling escalation. The boundaries could be instantiated in U.S. war plans, as well as by public statements that make the Chinese aware that the United States, while still capable of holding at risk targets throughout China, is not unnecessarily pursuing provocative attacks.

The boundaries in this situation might consist of restrictions such as an absolute prohibition on attacks on the mainland, an extremely restricted set of attacks designed to avoid triggering retaliatory attacks on sanctuary bases, or attacks limited against those units that have directly engaged U.S. forces. In all but the prohibition case, the onus is on the United States to correctly identify the threshold at which the Chinese would respond with attacks against U.S. bases and facilities, and then to stay below that threshold. Consequently, some risk of U.S. actions accidentally triggering escalation of the conflict through miscalculation would have to be accepted.

Render Irrelevant. A strategic move to render Chinese missile forces irrelevant to the successful execution of U.S. plans would likely alter basic objectives and timelines inside existing U.S. war plans. An example of such a strategy would be to minimize the prompt defense of Taiwan from all except direct invasion in favor of a long-war strategy against China that would allow the massing of superior U.S. forces and permit the United States to take the initiative at a time and place of its own choosing. Such an approach would accept that the missile forces could do damage early in a conflict, but that the United States would "ride out" the attacks and proceed with a deliberate campaign at the pace of its choosing. One could imagine that active defense of Taiwan might be limited to counterinvasion activities and that some mechanism for mitigating damage to material resources would be pursued in place of the precipitous introduction of forces vulnerable to missile attack.[39]

Render Ineffective. A strategic move to render the Chinese missile-centric force ineffective requires not so much a decision about basic strategy and approaches in a conflict, but a change in how current plans are executed and how the forces are equipped. This option does not describe a strategy but instead a set of prewar investment and deployment plans that would greatly decrease the impact of the Chinese missile forces. In this case, the key would be measures to protect installations from the impact of missile attacks through active and passive measures and, ideally, prevent the missiles from being launched in the first place through measures designed to either destroy or otherwise negate Chinese missile forces.

In many ways, the options of rendering ineffective can be thought of as a default U.S. position, since the bulk of U.S. plans could be kept pristine and the addition of defenses and alternate basing would allow for the United States to execute fully its plans in the event of a conflict. A practical example of U.S. operational level responses would be to harden airfields, disperse aircraft, procure and deploy missile defenses, and invest in more attrition reserves.

Escalation Dominance. The last option takes a page out of the Cold War playbook by suggesting a basic strategy of maintaining clear and absolute escalation dominance. Here the United States could implement a countervailing strategy that would hold at risk the entire spectrum of targets in China. In practice, this option would raise the possibility of a strategic campaign against China, including fairly comprehensive conventional military operations (air attacks, blockades, destruction of all Chinese nonnuclear power projection forces), and would retain the option of attacks on nuclear forces should the United States believe they were likely to be used. Nuclear forces would have to be prepared for limited nuclear options in

---

[39] Mitigation strategies designed to protect against physical damage might include options as diverse as passive hardening measures for high-value installations, subsidized war-risk insurance, replacement in-kind for lost defense items, or other financial mechanisms to lessen the impact of damage to important commercial and civil infrastructure.

response to selective Chinese attacks or a massive response should counter-value targets be attacked by the Chinese.

The escalation dominance strategy exploits the comprehensive military advantage enjoyed by the United States, but at the serious risk of unintended escalation and possible use of nuclear weapons. This is a relatively low-cost strategy in the sense that it requires little additional investment, but if things go wrong, the costs of miscalculation are extremely high for all concerned. Such an approach would seem to be attractive up and until the point deterrence has failed, and then the relatively automatic ratcheting up of the conflict would seem less attractive to both political and military decisionmakers. If escalation dominance was adopted as a bluff strategy (e.g., the United States had no real intention of fighting a conflict that way), it might face the unattractive possibilities of escalation for which it was in fact unprepared, ad hoc responses, or accepting a possibly serious reversal of its international interests.

Operational and Tactical Military Options

While the strategic options outlined above provide a glimpse of the rough set of avoidable policy options, many activities might take place within the context of the big strategies that fall into the realm of prudent military planning regardless of how the big strategy is formulated. All things being equal, it is better to have some protection from attack than it is to be vulnerable. The macro-strategy one selects frequently determines the degree to which protection plans are implemented.

Active and passive defense measures would be particularly useful in dealing with missile attack. Such protective measures include dispersal to prevent simple preplanned attacks, although its effects are relatively limited once the adversary has reliable, possibly near-real-time ISR available for targeting or smart munitions able to search over the dispersal locations. Sheltering helps by forcing the expenditure of an accurate penetrating weapon per sheltered aircraft. Shelters also allow for "goaltending"-type defenses to be used that might simply deflect or damage incoming weapons, causing them to impact ineffectually on the shelter. The issue of what to do with large aircraft on a base would require close examination, since protecting them by passive means such as shelters has always been problematic.

There are also active measures that can be used to enhance survivability of the forces. The three main methods are active missile defense, offensive counter-missile operations, and launch for survival. All of these options have strengths and weaknesses and are presented here to illustrate how a missile-centric force introduces trade-offs and added complexity to the conduct of U.S. military operations.

The first option is simply the application of missile defenses against Chinese missiles after they are launched against critical targets. Such a strategy may be useful if the target system is protected by missile defenses with several shot opportunities against the missiles and the target system can tolerate warheads leaking through the defenses.

Offensive counter-missile operations encompass the set of military tasks associated with striking by a variety of means at enemy missiles before they are launched. In the case of fixed sites, this is relatively straightforward. However, for mobile missiles it is a significant challenge to find the missiles prior to launch or even prosecute successful attacks against the transporter-erector-launcher after launch. This option requires very sophisticated and responsive ISR, as well as responsive strike capability to capitalize on fleeting detections. In addition, the option requires extensive operations over the Chinese mainland with all the attendant risks of escalation.

Another option for either actively or passively shielding U.S. forces from attack, or preventing an attack through preemption, is simply not being there when the attacking missiles arrive. For the vast bulk of the force, it would seem impractical to launch for survival. However, for a critical subset of forces, such an option might be attractive. Furthermore, high-demand assets might be airborne in any case and would be shielded against the worst of the effects.

A variant of the avoidance strategy is to use more remotely located bases and operating areas. Implicit in the remote basing option is the assumption that the number of missiles capable of attacking the bases is diminished sufficiently to make up for the added difficulty of operating at great distances from the point of conflict. In the case of airbases and aircraft carriers, this means tolerating the reduced sortie rate from the remote locations. However, as indicated earlier, this may only be a partial solution because long-range missile forces can be employed against even very distant bases to good effect if other protective measures have not been taken.

Signposts

If the Chinese were to produce a missile-centric force designed as a counter-transformational capability, how would the United States recognize this force, and could it be distinguished from missile forces designed to support a more conventional array of military operations? There are many possible indicators for missile-oriented activity, but there are only a few that would be helpful in distinguishing between the types of missile forces. The various signposts include declaratory statements, doctrinal developments, shifts in resource allocation, research and development interests, deployment patterns and numbers, testing, and exercises. Some of these are intended for the United States to observe, others are unavoidably observable with well-established and understood collection efforts, and some may need to be obtained through new collection methods.

Public and quasi-public statements, such as fairly accessible military writings on how the missile forces might be used, could provide some useful warning as to what the Chinese may be doing. Of particular interest would be the emergence of more explicit discussion of operations deep in enemy territory, and discussion of how those operations could have strategic effect on operations. Particular attention should be paid to counter-ISR and counter–strategic attack operations. Emergence of any discussion in these areas, when combined with programmatic changes, would be a helpful indicator of interest.

Another related tip-off would be active discussion of the significance of U.S. conventional strategic attacks. Here the key would be to look for a critical appraisal of the strengths and weaknesses of U.S. operations coming from groups not normally associated with protection of Chinese assets. In other words, look for the interest coming not from those concerned with PLA's ability to operate under attack but those associated with general military science and force employment issues.

A shift in resources toward long-range precision strike missile systems would be a significant indicator of potential interest in a missile-centric strategy. While the base technologies can be pursued in other missile programs, integration would require a reasonably sized development program that would need resources above and beyond that of any base missile program. However, as indicated earlier in this report, even a modest number of long-range conventional strike systems could have the effect desired by Chinese leaders. This means that a thorough understanding of the resources and programs needs to be developed to detect changes induced by additional demands for a conventional long-range missile force.

Observations on the research and development side will tend to be fairly difficult to sort from other existing long-range missile programs until systems are moving to the integration stage. The key here is to find the small set of key technologies of unique relevance to the capabilities needed for a missile-centric force. Understanding testing will be extremely important, since this will drive many conclusions. A clear understanding of how the Chinese approach testing and what they think can and cannot be accomplished via surreptitious testing will be vital.[40]

Deployment of key capabilities will be a clear indicator of interest in using these kinds of forces. However, ambiguity can be introduced by using systems associated with multiple missions and by avoidance of activities that clearly delineate which systems are being used for specific purposes. Actual use during an exercise would seem to be designed to intentionally signal the existence of a capability in a

---

[40] It is worth keeping in mind that there are different national styles to research and development, as well as acceptance of risk in development. It may be perfectly possible for China to field a system without adequate testing in order to throw U.S. planners off-balance, since the U.S. side may not be able to accept the possibility of the system working. However, this also means that Chinese decisionmakers might also have to accept a similar degree of uncertainty in regard to the performance of their weapon system and would be quite hesitant to count on its performance in combat.

quiet channel. The signaling would be intentional if the Chinese assumed they were being observed. Such open displays of capability are intended for both internal and external audiences. Finally, there would be the development of missile-centric unique supporting systems.

CHAPTER SEVEN

Option Four: Chinese Network-Centric Warfare

As previous chapters have argued, China can respond, if it so chooses, to the U.S. adoption of network-centric warfare in many ways. It can accelerate its conventional capabilities, enhance its ability to conduct irregular warfare, bolster its strategic forces, develop methods of countering U.S. networks directly, or adopt NCW itself. These responses are not mutually exclusive. One can buy more irregular and strategic warfare capabilities at the same time—but only if resources permit. Given limits on what China can invest in warfighting, they are competitive options, but not exclusive ones. To be sure, one would expect to see a heavy emphasis on C4ISR in a network-centric force just as one would expect to see a heavy emphasis on firepower in a conventional force. So, one can assess two different investment profiles and conclude that one is more network-centric than the other—but absolute assessments are simply unavailable. Even if the Chinese adopt NCW principles, their version of NCW warfare would not be the same as the U.S. version, and it might differ in some very particular ways.

What Would China's Version of NCW Look Like?

The seven major combatants of World War I—Germany, France, Britain, Austria, Italy, the United States, and even Russia—were of comparable population, per-capita income, technology, and philosophy. As a result, World War I had many symmetric elements, and when a new technology such as airplanes showed up on the battle-field, it was used in similar, if not identical ways by all sides. The United States and the Soviet Union were somewhat less symmetric. The two nations had similar populations and, in some technologies, were comparable, but the United States was much richer and opened up a sufficiently long lead in electronics; by the end of the Cold War, the conventional military contest had become one of superior technology versus superior numbers. Even so, the militaries of both countries had their doctrinal origins in the Western way of war.

Should the United States and China find themselves to be serious military competitors, there is every reason to believe that they would be quite different from each other thanks to different resource levels, geographies, strategic cultures, and legacy systems. The United States has developed its version of NCW to address its particular needs and opportunities. There is little reason to believe that the Chinese would develop something identical, or even very similar, to what the United States has created—even if both countries have access to the same commercial technologies. Warfighting doctrines, if meant to work rather than be fashionable, are necessarily solutions to certain politico-military problems, optimized in light of resources and endowments. The United States and China start off in far different places.

Indeed, "place" is one major difference. The United States is surrounded by unthreatening neighbors and large oceans; it goes abroad to fight and has had, and continues to have, access to overseas bases all over the world. China, although roughly as large in size, is a continental power with a small navy and very little power projection capability (or historic interest in having any, at least not since Zheng He's fleet was retired in the 1400s). It is surrounded by neighbors with whom it has had considerable "history." Chinese politico-military thought is dominated by two themes: its century-long (1839–1945) humiliation at the hands of the West (or a Westernized Japan) and its desire to recover Taiwan to restore its perceived territorial integrity.

Another difference is income. If China keeps growing at 6 percent per year while the U.S. economy grows at 3 percent, China's gross national product (GNP) will eventually overtake that of the United States, but this will occur far enough in the future to not be operationally relevant to more short-term scenarios. It is also likely that China's nominal GNP (i.e., what it is worth in terms of international purchases) is likely to lag its real GNP (based on domestic purchasing power). Even if China could afford to spend as much on defense as the United States does, its mix should reflect the fact that people are relatively cheap but foreign technology is relatively expensive. How cheap is another question. China shook off huge casualties in the Korean War, but, with incomes up and birth rates (apparently) below that of the United States, this profligacy is unlikely to be repeated. Conversely, it is hard to imagine that the PLA would make the kind of consistent effort the U.S. military does to save individual lives.

Strategic culture is another differentiator. Americans, for instance, see themselves as avoiding war unless provoked and then reacting by attempting to eliminate the enemy. When engaged, however, Americans feel disappointed at anything that leaves opponents intact. By contrast, since 1949, the goal has not necessarily been an annihilated opponent (although this option is not to be rejected if the opportunity presents itself) but to control the "overall strategic situation." Chinese leaders have viewed *all* military interventions since 1949 as successful in that they stabilized what they saw as deteriorating conditions. Therefore, threats to China's border integrity or the legitimacy of its ruling class are taken seriously—which is not the case in the United States. There is also the possibility that if China's central leadership is weak or the lines of authority are unclear, Chinese decisions may make sense only in terms of conflicts among bureaucratic elites (à la Japan circa 1941).

Other aspects of China's historical political culture present further differences with the United States. China grants concepts of hierarchy and bureaucracy far more respect than they merit in the United States (at least rhetorically). In what may appear to contradict this tendency, personal connections (*guanxi*) seem to play a larger role in decisionmaking than they (are supposed to) do here. On the gemeinschaft-gesellschaft continuum, China is closer to the former and the United States to the latter. This may introduce bias, affect how decisions get made, and thus how command and control systems are designed and used.

Legacy also matters. Since World War II, the United States has spent a few trillion dollars (at current prices) in building and operating the world's greatest air power. China has not. Having done so, the United States starts off with a large number of very sophisticated aircraft, an array of satellites, support facilities in all corners of the world, and a very deep manufacturing base. A great deal has also been learned in the process: how to build aircraft, integrate them and related defense systems, fly them, train people to fly and fix them, and use them to support warfighting objectives. The United States has very specific expectations of air power, not least of which has been that U.S. ground and naval troops are simply not shot at by enemy aircraft. It stands to reason that air power would be an important component of how the United States implements NCW.

But should China build that kind of air power? Absent a legacy base, the Chinese could well spend as much money as the United States does, yet they would do it far less efficiently (because of what they have yet to learn as well as their U.S. counterparts have) and when finished have, plane-for-plane, a less useful military establishment. China may simply not choose to put its money into competing that way. With, say UAVs or missiles, the legacy edge is smaller. So, if the Chinese seek to build network-centric forces around technologies in which the United States has not created such a large lead, they start on more even ground.

Conversely, it is by no means certain that the Chinese will innovate their way to a radically different version of NCW. The U.S. military is the gold standard for every military in the world and thus represents the model that they could aspire to, resources permitting, to prove themselves serious. Just as Japan industrialized in the 1950s and 1960s by copying the U.S. industrial base and innovating later, China first copies the U.S. military and innovates only after it has finished its education. A key difference was that Japanese and American businessmen were selling into the same global market. By contrast,

China and the United States are trying to solve different strategic problems.

Another way to illustrate the choices that China would have to make is to posit a typical NCW operation and ask whether the Chinese would invest in the capability to carry it out. Consider the following vignette: a company of soldiers is air-dropped tens or hundreds of kilometers behind enemy lines. Its mission is to seek out otherwise hard-to-find enemy assets (e.g., marshalling points), disrupt operations through quick attacks, and then finish the job by calling in firepower from over the horizon. Their job done, they are rapidly exfiltrated and return to base. Pulling off this scenario, however, has many prerequisites. First, there has to be a great deal of trust and initiative in this operation; once the company commander is out of sight, he is essentially on his own, and although there would be constant aural contact and even some visual confirmation, it is still not the same as being there. Second, success requires OTH fire support, which in turn calls for fires of sufficient range and precision and, no small thing, a command and control arrangement that gives the company commander confidence that the fires will be there when needed and not a minute later. Third, unless the company is completely on its own to seek out and dispatch the target on its own, one can expect a large amount of information exchange, especially tactical-level intelligence, especially over wireless links. Fourth, if the company will be operating for more than a day or two, it will need more logistics than it can comfortably pack for; hence, air resupply as needed. This requires some degree of air superiority. Fifth, exfiltration (and not necessarily always when scheduled) will probably require the use of rotary aircraft; doing so safely would require similar air superiority.

Are the Chinese up to this kind of operation? Does their military culture support long, untethered operations with little direct supervision well? Are they willing to put very sensitive information out in the field and trust that it is exchanged securely—and with the right parties (the risk of capture is not a trivial one in this vignette)? Will they be willing to scrub the operation and take the risks in pulling their warfighters out if their lives are in danger? Last, are they sufficiently confident in their air capabilities to conduct an operation in which so much depends on their ability to deliver, supply, and re-cover individuals using aircraft that are anything but stealthy?

Having established the prima facie case that China's version of NCW may differ from the U.S. version, can one say what these dif-ferences would entail?

Specific Chinese Characteristics of NCW

The Chinese are likely to bring into their version of NCW the ten-dencies that they have long exhibited in their history and military.

One strong theme is control over information. Chinese strategic culture holds no affirmative belief in the right of people to have information. Hence their largely successful approach to censoring the Internet (as befits a society in which bureaucratic status was corre-lated with a knowledge of literature). Operational security (OPSEC)—the belief that it is both worthwhile and achievable—is also a leitmotif of the PLA. As a national army, the PLA went to war three times: in Korea (1950), India (1962), and Vietnam (1979). In all three cases, the Chinese actions were a complete surprise and they managed to catch their opponents off guard. In the case of Korea, China managed to infiltrate 200,000 "volunteers" into the theater before it was obvious how many there were and what they were there to do. All three invasions were also accompanied by meticulous plan-ning (although operations against the United States and Vietnam were confounded with less-than-perfect intelligence on the adversary).

Emphasizing OPSEC and planning suggests that the Chinese will tend toward the concentrated approach, certainly at the grand-strategy level, and perhaps also at the level of implementation. Even if China's use of information technology were to reach U.S. standards, it is hard to imagine the Chinese adopting a peer-to-peer messaging system for troops to coordinate with one another. This reluctance may even extend to their reluctance to field distributed sensors on the theory that every captured sensor is just one more intelligence loss that not only gives away their plans but also reveals their technologi-cal capabilities (or lack thereof). Similarly, the Chinese emphasis on computer operational security may make them extremely loathe to open up files to inquiry or to link their systems with those of their allies and enable the latter to take advantage of China's information capabilities.

Other current tendencies of the PLA may also be worked into its conception of NCW. As if they had inherited as much from the Red Army, the Chinese are particularly fond of rockets and artillery, as well as electronic warfare, and, of late, CNA. They may find attractive the notion of feeding sensor-derived target coordinates into their precision-guided rockets and thereby trying to control the battlefield through volleys of precision fires.

China's relative backwardness at systems integration skills, however, leaves several dilemmas that it must resolve before it can claim to have implemented NCW. One is the choice of tight versus loose systems integration. Tight systems integration is characteristic of such platforms as aircraft; the Web, when it works, is an example of loose systems integration. The plain fact is that the Chinese are not very good at the former, but are very nervous of having to depend on the latter. The result may be that the Chinese use people in situations where the United States would use software to glue its systems together. This would lend their systems a certain robustness, but at the expense of responsiveness. The other dilemma is in how they would supply precision-guided munitions (PGMs) to war. The basic choice is between buying (1) expensive ISR that is good enough to guide cheap munitions to the target, (2) inexpensive ISR with PGMs that boast sophisticated guidance and control, or (3) inexpensive ISR with enough munitions to tolerate otherwise unacceptably low probability of kill. The first path requires a high order of systems integration skills; the second, expertise at precision manufacturing; and the third, experience at running logistics systems. Not one of the three is a Chinese specialty.

Might the PLA rise above its history and its cultural baggage? The PLA could adopt style of NCW that is highly distributed and exploits its commercial success to substitute myriads of cheap commercial-grade sensors and weapons for the U.S. model of sophistication everywhere. Some indicators of that shift would be a corresponding emergence of such thinking in research papers coming out of China's military institutions, growing links between the PLA and commercial manufacturing industries (especially in southern China and Korea), a demonstrated willingness (e.g., in exercises) to treat sensors as expendables, and an emphasis on software and systems integration. Other indicators would be evident in what they chose to *de*-emphasize: artillery units and the U.S. military as a focus of emulation.

How Their NCW Might Affect Ours

Since the end of the Cold War, the U.S. search for ever-greater military effectiveness has proceeded without the spur of direct competition. Although the United States has responded to capabilities (e.g., Scud missiles, chemical weapons) presented by miscellaneous adversaries, development has been driven more by what technology has permitted than by what foes have compelled. China, should it choose to compete with the United States, has the resources to reintroduce the element of direct military competition, in which some aspect of NCW, if not the whole approach, is likely to be a major component of whatever it does. To the extent that is so, what should that do to the U.S. development trajectory? If the Chinese get to a point in which they can see more of the battlefield, in finer detail, and more persistently—coupled with weaponry that can be aimed to a moving spot on the map—a war's odds would revolve around the exploitation and avoidance of signature rather than force concentration. This has several ramifications.

The U.S. version of NCW, for instance, emphasizes the cycle-time dominance that comes from wide and robust connections among warfighters and other decisionmakers. This emphasis has two components: thinking faster than foes and outmaneuvering them. Faster thinking is not going out of style, but evidence that adversaries in war are locked in tight real-time action-reaction cycles is intermittent at best. Far more time is spent getting the parts of complicated plans—the nature of which are only vaguely visible to the other side—to come together, against which the enemy is but one obstacle. The role of outmaneuvering is in doubt. Raw speed is losing its edge. Warfighters cannot outrun light and hence cannot avoid surveillance simply by moving faster; most platforms cannot outrun the PGMs that would be used to go after them.

To the extent that cycle-time matters in an environment in which both sides have "staring" ISR, of greatest importance is the contest both sides face between exposure time and prosecution time. Exposure time is the gap between when something creates signature and when it can return to cover or invisibility. Smaller gaps are better. Prosecution times come from what is required to find, classify, verify, geolocate, engage, and fly out to a target. Hence, a new rationale for electronic warfare, information warfare, and deception: They lengthen the time required for finding, classifying, and verifying. Similarly, the virtue of loitering weapons is that they shorten the fly-out component of the engagement cycle.

Error control (and exploitation) is an important component of signature control (and exploitation). To err is human, but as Steven Biddle's work (on two wars in Iraq and one in Afghanistan) suggests, it is increasingly fatal. When facing modern forces, it is not only inadvisable to generate detectable signature but also to execute operations in a sloppy and uncoordinated manner that leave things undone or too messy, leave oneself heir to faults that cause further faults, or even to guess wrong about what the enemy will do. Hitherto, warfighters might have been able to detect mistakes themselves and clean them up while the enemy had little idea what was going on; increasingly, such mistakes are now likely to be detected and broadcast by enemy forces faster and with graver consequences. As such, in battle between peers without surprises, outcomes favor those who make fewer errors. The importance of avoiding error lends importance to education and training, something at which U.S. forces excel. Nevertheless, they must learn to err less often and find ways to detect and recover from errors before others exploit them.

Often, one cannot help but generate signature, and as Chinese capabilities improve, the signature threshold goes down. One of the tenets of NCW is that it is good to disperse forces (while using command and control to maintain concentration of fires). To the extent that masses of people are hard to hide, it helps to make sure they need not congregate. Sufficiently dispersed people, particularly in settled areas, can blend into the background. The story is different for equipment. As China adopts NCW, it is likely to be able to spot massed formations of platforms. Dispersal would be important; after all, massed military platforms are unlike anything else (by comparison, Boeing 747s do not fly in squadrons). But as China's C4ISR continues to improve, it then gains the ability to detect and characterize specific military assets. Warships are not detected because they steam in battle groups but because they do not look or sail like cargo carriers. As they do get this ability, the viability of individual platforms is open to question, and the strategy of protecting them by not massing them would offer diminishing returns.

Conclusions

Will the Chinese adopt network-centric warfare? Regardless of whether they adopt our brand of NCW, it is likely that they will enhance their investment in sensors and precision weapons. The upshot of that development is straightforward. If our NCW makes the battlefield visible to us, theirs is likely to make the battlefield visible to them. In particular, that means our own forces will be more visible to them and thus more likely to be targets. The more visible the battlefield, and the more that visibility is tantamount to destruction, the more difficult it will be to go to war with platforms. The U.S. response to that may be to accelerate certain aspects of its NCW evolution toward deploying sensors and weapons from a distance, and, if it must operate closely, to do so either with no signature (i.e., stealth) or with so much signature as to be disorienting. In either case, exposure times must be short. Both sides, China and the United States, may pursue the informatization of warfare to its logical conclusion. Victory, if not inherent in the balance of forces or unique attributes of geography, falls to whoever has the best combination of surprise, error control, fortune, and highly trained people. Ironically, a confrontation between two technologically advanced, network-centric militaries would likely reduce the importance of technology in favor of people and their ability to make rapid but accurate decisions with incomplete or overwhelming amounts of information. In such a contest, volunteer military personnel drawn from an open, educated society like that of the United States would appear to have the advantage over a stovepiped military embedded in an authoritarian state, but the blinding pace of social, cultural, and technological change in China strongly suggests that this conclusion will not always remain true.

Enhancing or Even Transcending Network-Centric Warfare?

Enhancing Network-Centric Warfare

So, are platforms doomed? The short answer is inevitably, but only if China (or some equally well-endowed competitor) adopts the basic elements of network-centric warfare (NCW), and not without some false remissions.

Platforms have three enduring advantages over dismounted infantry: they are armored, they carry armament, and they transport forces and firepower. One cannot sail or fly without them. The armor increases the size of weapon required to kill it. The mobility and armament give its owner the power to place weapons closer to their targets. Yet, ultimately, the viability of platforms depends on the comparative economics of protection vis-à-vis destruction. Here, economics favors the weapon. Armor and mobility may render cheap weapons impotent, but their contribution to the cost of an advanced weapon is more modest. For precision-guided munitions (PGMs) in the $100,000 to $1,000,000 class, warheads and propulsion constitute only 10 to 20 percent of the cost; guidance and control constitutes the rest. But as a military's intelligence, surveillance, and reconnaissance (ISR) gets better, the need for sophisticated guidance and control goes down. Information provided to the munition or inherent in its flight profile gets the PGM close enough to the target that its subsequent search space is small; for Joint Direct Attack Munitions (JDAMs), it is nonexistent. Perhaps platforms may improve their armor or speed to defeat PGMs, but the economics of doing so may be disappointing. Improvements in ISR mean that PMGs can work with cheaper guidance-and-control units, thereby saving enough money to afford larger warheads and more powerful propulsion systems to defeat such strategies. Armor itself is not free and the cost of moving extra weight creates requirements for larger engines and more complex logistics.

Forcing attackers to fire from farther away increases the fly-out time and thus gives the platform a little more time to disappear or evade being hit. But in the end, in a contest between platforms and weapons, victory goes to whoever runs out of stuff last, and the economics for platforms—unless they *do* become harder to find—are becoming increasingly dismal.[1]

Throughout this period, two transitions merit note: from unitary to distributed sensors and from manned to unmanned platforms. Distributed sensors offer the possibility that, with sufficient production volumes, their price can cross the chasm between expensive mil-spec items and inexpensive civilian items. Although the latter are not likely to be as environmentally hardened or individually robust, if there are enough of them and provision has been made for redundant coverage, some failure can be tolerated. Distributed sensors also permit finer coverage, closer to the source; for instance, they can be deployed to areas that, to a single-point sensor, sit in the "shadows." Best of all, their numbers can exceed what the enemy can destroy one

---

[1] Can directed-energy weapons used to shoot at incoming missiles save the platform? The Israelis have proven (with the help of U.S. technology) that an expensive immobile laser can destroy a light cheap rocket such as a Kytusha. Yet further progress must face the fact that a laser is only as good as its pointing accuracy, its chemistry, and its ability to overcome countermeasures. Pointing accuracy is bound to improve, but at far distances there is no way to overcome the effect of atmospheric distortion on the beam. Counting on improvements in chemistry (rather than, say, electronics) to make a weapon system viable is proposition that must overcome chemistry's maturity as a science. Countermeasures typically receive little attention until the measure itself is near deployment. PGMs could be redesigned so as to deflect or shed energy more easily. Or PGMs could be clustered so that a directed-energy weapon cannot get enough energy on each and every incoming between when each PGM comes in range to the time it hits (therefore, clustering PGMs does require tight coordination and timing and thus is unsuitable for any of the swarming metaphors that are bandied about for such weapons).

by one. A large expensive sensor has to protect itself because so much rests on it, and single-point failures attract adversary attention. Unitary sensors have some economies of their own. There are often economies of scale for building large units (e.g., the cost of a power generating unit does not double when its power output does). Best of all, unitary sensors do not have to establish and maintain the complex communications mesh that distributed sensors do. The communications that is required to coordinate and harvest the results from many small sensors is not only difficult to program but may be interfered with—another irresistible temptation. On net, the odds favor distributed sensors as experience builds on how to write software to manage and coordinate them, especially in the face of electronic warfare.

Having sensed the target, how would one hit it in an enhanced NCW environment? The problem of hitting fixed points with a munition is essentially a solved one; since they do not move, fly-out time is not an issue. But mobile targets have to be hit when visible and within range.[2] If the visibility time is short, one must either use fast munitions or keep munitions on call close to the target (engaged forces do this very well by shooting at what is shooting at them). Speed is expensive; the cost increment to go from current speeds of Mach 2 to 3 to something twice as fast may be steep, and such munitions may not be easy to steer against moving targets. Nothing is faster than directed-energy weapons, but even if they can be made to work, they are limited to line-of-sight engagements.

To put weapons closer to the target, one could implant them in place beforehand, fly them out in their own orbits, or collect them and put them on loitering weapons carriers. As with mines, implanting them generally requires one owns the terrain in advance and has enough confidence that these weapons will not die, drift, or be discovered in the meantime (or put locals at risk after the war ends).

---

[2] The problem of hitting a *hard* fleeting target may also be addressed by first sending out a fast or close munition to hit it in such a way as to leave a persistent signature or at least slow it down. After that, it might be a mobile target but not a fleeting target. Subsequent rounds to defeat the target's hardness would not have to operate under the tight time constraints that the first round did.

This does not apply for engagements over water, in enemy territory, or anywhere that control shifts unexpectedly from one to the other side. As for weapons carriers on call, large bombers performed that role in Operation Iraqi Freedom. But how much longer should such carriers be manned? The U.S. Air Force has shown considerable interest in unmanned combat aerial vehicles (UCAVs) performing exactly that role, but analysis suggests that there is little to be gained from building UCAVs that mirror the capabilities and parameters of manned aircraft, notably a full set of self-defense measures. UCAVs do not need environmental conditioning and can pull more than the 9Gs that pilots are limited to, but taking people out of the cockpit increases the requirements for high-bandwidth communications. If, however, designers exploit the fact that UCAVs are no more worth protecting than an equivalent expenditure on munitions, it may be possible to dispense with many of the aircraft's self-protection features and realize radically different economics compared with manned aircraft. More of them would be lost in every type of threat environment, but they can be fielded in larger numbers.

What role, therefore is left for people on the scene once NCW is enhanced? Generally, the more mechanized a warfare task is, the more easily the people element can be removed (e.g., as it already is in space). Those tasks in war that require seeing things more than a few meters away and subsequently destroying them can, in the long run, almost always be done more efficiently by breaking the job up into seeing and striking, carried out respectively through sensors and PGMs. For the most part, seeing and striking are the primary missions of the Air Force, the Navy, and the mechanized branches of the Army and Marine Corps.

Yet people can do some things better than sensors and weapons. They can scrutinize and threaten other people from arbitrarily close distances. Even in the first Gulf War, Iraqi forces dwindled but did not bolt until they perceived that they were going to be overrun (hiding against manned aircraft, not to mention sensors, is still easier than hiding against someone who can bring a tank up close). In Kosovo, NATO forces could easily hit fixed targets but not Serbian tanks (even if the Serbs got little use out of such tanks). In Operation

Enduring Freedom, nascent techniques of enhanced NCW multiplied the forces of the Northern Alliance, but there still had to be local forces to be multiplied. The trick is keeping one's own ground forces intact in the face of the other side's NCW.

Similarly, people are good at scouring for other people and small objects, because they can bring their eyes and ears indefinitely close to an object as needed. If nothing else, personal observation allows the interpretation of what sensors report to be calibrated to reality. A great deal of information gathering is also engaging with and talking to other people. There is no feasible way today, or most likely even 20 years hence, that a Saddam Hussein could have been found without at least some people on the ground. Similarly, forces on the ground are necessary to interact with those who already live there: other militaries, intelligence sources, or everyday citizens.

But note that most of these roles are already played by dismounted warfighters. Many of these functions are already assigned to special operators explaining, in part, the growth of that community—one unlikely to be supplanted by the more mechanical elements of enhanced NCW.

Transcending NCW

The dilemmas of modern warfare may be reflected in the child's game of rock-paper-scissors. The mechanization of warfare in the 19th and 20th centuries signified the ascension of machines over man. Although the reality on the battlefield is complex, as a rule platform-supported forces outfought dismounted ones; therefore, platforms were bought whenever countries could afford to (rock over scissors). Yet by being distinct, platforms can be targeted. The informatization of warfare is elevating the role of sensors and weapons above that of platforms (paper over rock). Ironically, it is far harder to target individuals, such as dismounted infantry and special operators. As warfare becomes less a matter of brute force and more a matter of psychology and persuasion, one sees the re-ascendancy of the individual (scissors over paper). Saddam's tanks could cow unhappy Iraqis, and our

NCW could blow Saddam's tanks away, but our problem is that unhappy Iraqis could bring our mission in Iraq to failure.

Enhanced NCW may represent the apotheosis of conventional warfare, but the techniques of conventional warfare may not necessarily address the nation's national security problems. Even China—a country that may soon afford to play in our league—may conclude that it cannot go to war in platforms and thus may be impelled to going to war by using people and things (e.g., pickup trucks) that being indistinguishable from commercial life do not stand out as targets. This is not the only future. Changes in technology that render some of the above assumptions about seeing and hitting cannot be ruled out. Nevertheless, asymmetric foes are adopting such methods, and if they appear effective against the United States, more symmetric foes may well follow.

So, for the United States, the fundamental problem—the one that forces us to transcend[3] NCW—is finding soldiers in the shadows. In the 21st century, it may become very difficult to distinguish adversaries from the population, if soldiers prefer to fight there. Warfighters, when not identified as such, can more easily get to where they are going and credibly deny affiliation with enemies of defenders. Terrorists have shown that a few individuals can do great damage, if by nothing else forcing others to invest time and attention to counter them. Support warfighters have it even easier; the tools of their trade are not incriminating, per se. The more globalization, the less that large numbers of foreigners excites suspicion.

---

[3] Transcending NCW does not mean getting past networking. Shared situational awareness remains important, both for military operations and for commercial ones (e.g., Wal-Mart and Dell). People will (rightfully) expect to be networked wherever they are, and it will only become cheaper to do so. Despite the 2000–2002 downturn in telecommunications investment, infrastructure continues to advance. Even in the United States, tens of millions of people have broadband. The emergence of Wi-Fi (wireless fidelity) and successors (e.g., WiMAX) should offer such connectivity to the mobile. Networking has its problems—spam (or simply information overload)—and operational security will persist even after improvements in operating systems have put paid to worms and viruses. Networking may also be increasingly driven by the proliferation of radio-frequency identification (RFID) devices. Cheap disposable sensors are becoming commonplace, and the percentage of network traffic created by communications among devices is likely to continue to rise. Powerful data-mining algorithms will be slower in coming, but come they will.

The challenge, therefore, is to identify such people beforehand. Timing really matters if the role of shadow soldiers is to pave the way for a rapid insertion of regular units rather than wreak randomly timed destruction.

From Seeing Everything to Knowing Everyone

The goal of identifying everyone with whom one has or would come into contact is analogous to the goal, enunciated by Admiral Owens, former Chairman of the Joint Chiefs of Staff, in the mid-1990s, of knowing everything that sits or moves in the battlespace (a cube 200 nautical miles on each side). In many ways, the techniques for doing so are the same. NCW relies on persistent ISR. When an object exposes itself as being sufficiently different from the background of commercial life, or as associated with hostile activity, it is to be identified as such, geolocated, tracked (if moving), and dealt with. Similarly, to find the hidden enemy, it may be necessary to create a system of persistent monitoring that can pick out those unauthorized for a given area or activity, or who are associated with hostile activity (e.g., preparations made in advance of a terrorist attack).

Again, by comparison to battlefield surveillance, any computer-assisted technique for identifying things or people who are out of place requires sophisticated techniques of data mining and pattern recognition. To work well, however, such techniques must be coupled with methods that get everything to reveal itself. In NCW, the movement of troops is a forcing function. When looking for specific individuals, something comparable—e.g., active searching and questioning—may be necessary. In both cases, the targets of search have to learn how to avoid mistakes and adopt deceptive covers. The hunters must detect mistakes quickly and see through deception. In the long run, success goes to whoever learns fastest, but unless one invests heavily in forcing functions, pursuers must be patient.

Is it necessary to know who *everyone* is,[4] or is it sufficient to be able to distinguish those who belong from those who do not? The latter is the real goal, but, as a practical matter, the former may be required of the latter. Were one able to classify individuals on sight (e.g., by their wearing insignia) then everyone else can be quickly screened out. Alternatively if the number of authorized people is contained, the human eyeball can pick out the rest—but eyeballs do not scale well past a few hundred.

More typically, when scanning large populations, several search rules may be needed—and they all indicate that as many people as possible be specifically identifiable. First, separating out those you know from those you do not know permits one to more closely scrutinize the latter; this applies both before anything happens and afterward. For example, in a video of people leaving the scene, if there are ten individuals, nine of whom are known are unlikely to have been the one, then the attention focuses on the tenth. Second, many attributes of malevolence are tied to patterns of association or behavior, which cannot be analyzed without gathering such information (even if immediately discarded on inspection) from everyone. Third, one may have intelligence on adversaries that can be used to distinguish them from the rest of the population at certain points, but this can only be checked if similar data can be captured from everyone at such points (by contrast, if there are only one or two persons in question and it is easy to pick them out by looking at them, then the only "data" that is collected on everyone else comes from the fact that

---

[4] In cases where attackers may be recruited from the population at large (admittedly, a minor factor in these scenarios), defenders intent on knowing who everyone is can foster the impression that one's comings and goings are closely scrutinized and that everyone's friends and relatives have been identified in advance. All this raises the odds of detection and punishment for doing or even taking steps to do something harmful. Conversely, knowledge about individuals is the first step in crafting appeals to each of them in favor of staying out of trouble, supporting authorities, and providing intelligence on those who are planning on getting into trouble. The Panopticon effect—the belief that one is always being watched by authorities—is necessarily an illusion that may be violated the first time someone gets away with something. Since the Panopticon effect relies in large part on this belief not being questioned, authorities may want to convey the sense that just because they do not take action against every offense, even major ones, does not mean they do not have a more strategic and subtle plan to make use of the data at other times or in other ways.

someone is looking at them long enough to make that determination).

Knowing who people are does not obviate the value of today's menu of counter-irregular techniques, but it bolsters them and permits new ones. All this assumes that when it actually comes to the point of combat, the authorities can quickly bring more force to bear than the irregulars can.

What kind of identity can one acquire? The best is accurate identity: a one-to-one correlation between an individual and an identity from birth onward. The second-best is consistent identity: a one-to-one correlation between an individual and an identity from some point, such as enrollment, onward. Hostile outsiders, perhaps needless to add, will rarely have the best identity documents (e.g., China will not be handing over birth records to Taiwan), so having the best on everyone else is of considerable help.

There are many contributors to someone's identity. One is a person's name (and correlated attributes such as a social security number). For most of us, law-abiding as we are, there will be a lifetime-long consistency in the name we use and thus the records we leave under that name. Even malevolent people often use their real names because they believe, not without cause, that it will not hurt them: either the authorities have little intelligence on them or there are no mechanisms to link the use of their name to whatever alerts exist on them (as was the case for the 19 hijackers).

Second are the relationships—relatives and friends—that one has. Some of these relationships are permanent. Even if they do not indicate someone's current behavior, they do characterize who a person really is.

Third, a person may be characterized by a history of transactions. Many of those who change their name to avoid getting caught have nevertheless established such a trail that may link their name, relationships, habits, and even pictures.

All three—name, relationships, and transactions—are probabilistic and temporary forms of identity. One can change a name, avoid one's relatives, make new friends, and engage in a completely different set of transactions. Yet for most of us, they are strong clues to who we are, and even those who assume a new identity cannot always drop all remnants of the old one.

A fourth, or at least more measurable, indicator of identity is someone's biometrics. Biometrics have the advantage that they are stable over time and difficult to shed. Some biometrics are so unique that getting them makes it possible to guess who the person in question is absent further information; conversely, it makes it very difficult for one person to assume two identities if such biometrics are both in the database.[5] Fingerprints, DNA, and, irises (maybe) fit in this category. Other biometrics, such as a person's face, handprint, voice, or signature, are not unique enough to establish an identity but are good enough to validate one (e.g., if someone gets an ID card with a picture on it, the next person who presents that ID card and looks like the picture will probably and reasonably be accepted as that person—even if an organization large enough to have many people who look the same can sometimes fool this validation method).

Checking someone's biometrics is obtrusive, however, and usually requires the person's consent. It cannot be done too often or where this is not an obvious requirement of passage. One can ask for identification without complaint for every border crossing, but not for every street crossing.

Only a few biometrics can be collected unobtrusively, notably a person's face, but it is an unreliable indicator of identity unaided. This is where all the other personal and transaction information helps. If one sees a group, and can identify one or two people, some combination of facial photographs and known relationships helps in guessing who the rest are. The same, albeit with less confidence, can be said for participants at a transaction. The data presented can permit a guess. For those who turn up blanks or where greater certainty

---

[5] Exactly which biometrics establish uniqueness is by no means settled. One wants to avoid false positives—a person whose biometrics is close enough to another's as to engender misplaced suspicion that he or she is registering twice. As a rule, the number of false positives rises with the square of the population enrolled. Thus a technique that could be useful in Taiwan might lead to problems if applied throughout all of China.

is required—one hopes, a small percentage of the time—more direct queries may be called for.

Generating identification cards should help. The process of enrollment is not only an opportunity to collect biometric data (a process that only has to be undergone once) but it can be used to provide an association between a biometric and an identification number. Such numbers, if used in transactions (and there are many ways to make this the preferred method) can permit a large number of transactions to be recorded into a database. One could also build RFIDs into identification cards that can let them be used readily for transactions. There may also be ways to engineer identification cards so that they can be queried unobtrusively at a distance. One can electronically query the person (on the assumption that a card is being carried), read the identification number, crosswalk the number to biometrics information, pull up a picture of a face and other relationship data, and then determine whether the face that has the card is the face in the database. The more transactions and other information are associated with an identity, the greater the confidence one can have in any guess of who someone is. That said, there are venues, such as a crowded train station, in which there are few if any clues on who might be there in the first place.

It would be ironic, however, if measures to improve the efficacy of fighting irregulars so alienate the population as to produce irregulars themselves. Many factors will influence whether such a regime would set off a backlash: the sociopolitical culture of the country where a surveillance regime is imposed, the situation there (a country afraid of and mobilized against outsiders might be more tolerant), how disruptive a surveillance regime may be, the rules under which it is run, and who runs it. A surveillance regime run by the U.S. military with no end date and no accountability that creates hassles and reduces dignity in a country where privacy is prized and threat levels from the outside are low is likely to have problems. One run by locals (albeit with U.S. technical assistance) that is limited in time and scope, circumspect and respectful, in a place where public order is prized and threat levels from outside are considered high is more likely to be accepted, perhaps even valued. To quote the U.S. Marine

Corps' *Small Wars Manual* (1940, p. 25): "It has been found that the average native is not only willing and anxious but proud to carry some paper signed by a military authority to show that he is recognized."

Finally, it is worth remembering that such a surveillance system is unlikely to go away just because U.S. forces do. However, such information may make it easier for local governments to control crime and administer social programs. Yet many of the governments we might help are not necessarily the most civil-liberties conscious. The United States might be able to remove the sensors and data-mining algorithms that make the system efficient. But taking home individual records (e.g., of biometrics, relationships, transactions) is another thing. Such a threat may well de-energize, if not enrage, the locals that we would count on to administer the program while we are there.

References

Allen, Ken, and Maryanne Kivlehan, "Implementing PLA Second Artillery Doctrinal Reforms," paper presented at the RAND/CNAC PLA conference, Washington, D.C., December 2002.

Asian Development Bank, "People's Republic of China," in *Asian Development Outlook 2003*, Hong Kong: Oxford University Press, 2003. Online at www.adb.org/Documents/Books/ADO/2003/prc.asp (as of January 12, 2005).

Baker, John, and Kevin J. Pollpeter, "Red Dragon on the Rise? Strategic Implications of the Chinese Human Space Flight Program," *Space News*, December 19, 2004, p. 19.

"Beijing Arrests Military Officers on Spy Charges," *China Post*, April 17, 2004. "Blockade and Kill Taiwan Independence's 'Aegis'," *Xiandai Bingqi*, January 2, 2003, pp. 41–44 [in FBIS as "PRC: Joint Tactics for Destroying 'Aegis,' 'Arleigh Burke' Described," January 2, 2003, FBIS document CPP20030409000179].

Bottelier, Peter, "How Stable Is China? An Economic Perspective," in David L. Shambaugh, ed., *Is China Unstable? Assessing the Factors*, Armonk, N.Y.: M. E. Sharpe, 2000, pp. 63–78.

Bradsher, Keith, "A Logjam for Transportation in China," *New York Times*, March 5, 2004, p. C1.

Brown, Harold, Joseph W. Prueher, and Adam Segal, *Chinese Military Power*, New York: Council on Foreign Relations, 2003.

Chase, Michael, and Evan Medeiros, "China's Evolving Nuclear Calculus: Modernization and the Doctrinal Debate," paper presented at RAND/CNAC PLA conference, Washington, D.C., December 2002.

Chen Fangyou (陈访友), *Naval Campaign Teaching Materials* (海军战役学教程), Beijing: National Defense University Press, 1991.

Chen Huan, "The Third Military Revolution," in Michael Pillsbury, ed., *Chinese Views of Future Warfare*, Washington, D.C.: National Defense University Press, 1998.

Cheng, Dean, "The Chinese Space Program: A 21st Century Fleet in Being," in James C. Mulvenon and Andrew N.D. Yang, *A Poverty of Riches: New Challenges and Opportunities in PLA Research*, Santa Monica, Calif.: RAND Corporation, CF-189-NSRD, 2003, pp. 25–48.

Chongqing Ribao (Chongqing Daily).

"China Advised to Keep an Eye on Fiscal Deficit," *People's Daily Online*, December 27, 2002. Online at http://english.people.com.cn/200212/27/eng20021227_109173.shtml (as of February 2005).

"China Bank Bailout Could Need US$290 Bln: Report," *People's Daily Online*, January 27, 2003. Online at http://english.peopledaily.com.cn/200301/27/eng20030127_110839.shtml (as of February 2005).

"China Detains Two More Taiwanese Suspected of Espionage," Agence France-Presse, February 13, 2004.

"Chinese Mainland Smashes Taiwan Spy Ring," Xinhua, December 24, 2003.

Christensen, Thomas J., "China," in Richard J. Ellings and Aaron J. Friedberg, eds., *Strategic Asia 2002–2003: Asian Aftershocks*, Seattle: National Bureau of Asian Research, 2002.

Cliff, Roger, *The Military Potential of China's Commercial Technology*, Santa Monica, Calif.: RAND Corporation, MR-1292-AF, 2001.

Cui Changqi (崔长崎), *21st Century Air Attacks and Counter Air Attacks* (二十一世纪空袭与反空袭), Beijing: PLA Press, 2002.

Dai Qingmin (戴清民), ed., *Introduction to Information Operations* (信息作战概论), Beijing: PLA Press, 1999.

Downs, Erica Strecker, *China's Quest for Energy Security*, Santa Monica, Calif.: RAND Corporation, MR-1244-AF, 2000.

"Espionage, Corruption Cases in China, Dec 03–Feb 04," *BBC Monitoring International Reports*, February 14, 2004.

Foreman, William, "Taiwan Arrests Military Officer on Spy Charges—The Third Such Case in Month," Associated Press, December 3, 2003.

"Former Taiwan Spy Chief Denies Leaking Secrets During His Four Years in China," *TaiwanNews.com* (Associated Press), April 14, 2004. Online at http://www.etaiwannews.com/Taiwan/2004/04/14/1081907696.htm (as of February 2005).

Gellman, Barton, "U.S. and China Nearly Came to Blows in '96; Tension Over Taiwan Prompted Repair of Ties," *Washington Post*, June 21, 1998, p. A1.

Gill, Bates, James Mulvenon, and Mark Stokes, "The Chinese Second Artillery Corps: Transition to Credible Deterrence," in James C. Mulvenon and Andrew N.D. Yang, eds., *The People's Liberation Army as Organization: Reference Volume v1.0*, Santa Monica, Calif.: RAND Corporation, CF-182-NSRD, 2002, pp. 510–581.

Gordon, Michael, "Secret U.S. Study Concludes Taiwan Needs New Arms," *New York Times*, April 1, 2001, p. A1.

Guo Xilin, "The Aircraft Carrier Formation Is Not an Unbreakable Barrier," *Guangming Ribao*, December 26, 2000 [in FBIS as "PRC Article Describes Shortcomings of Aircraft Carrier Formations," December, 29, 2000, FBIS document CPP20001229000036)].

He Dingqing, *A Course on the Science of Campaigns* (战役学教程), Beijing: Military Science Press, 2001.

Hsu, Brian, "Petty Officer Gets Life Sentence," *Taipei Times*, December 18, 2002, p. 3. Online at www.taipeitimes.com/News/taiwan/archives/2002/12/18/187627 (as of February 2005).

Jiang Lei (蒋磊), *Modern Strategy for Using the Inferior to Defeat the Superior* (现代以劣胜优战略), Beijing: National Defense University Press, 1997.

Johnston, Alastair Iain, "China's New 'Old Thinking': The Concept of Limited Deterrence," *International Security*, Vol. 20, No. 3, Winter 1995/96, pp. 5–42.

_____, "Prospects for Chinese Nuclear Force Modernization: Limited Deterrence Versus Multilateral Arms Control," *China Quarterly*, No. 146, June 1996, pp. 548–576

Kahn, Joseph, "China Gambles on Big Projects for Its Stability," *New York Times*, January 13, 2003a, p. A1.

_____, "Chinese Officers Say Taiwan's Leaders Are Near 'Abyss of War'," *New York Times*, December 4, 2003b, p. A7.

Kynge, James, "Rural Poverty May Threaten China's Future, Zhu Warns National People Congress," *Financial Times*, March 6, 2003, p. 11.

Lardy, Nicholas R., "Sources of Macroeconomic Instability in China," in David L. Shambaugh, ed., *Is China Unstable? Assessing the Factors*, Armonk, N.Y.: M. E. Sharpe, 2000, pp. 57–62.

Li Bin, "Nuclear Weapons and International Relations" (核武器与国际关系), briefing presented at the Beijing Student Doctoral Student Union Academic Lecture Series, Beijing University, November 25, 2003.

Li Hechun and Yourong Chen, "Sky War: A New Form of War That Might Erupt in the Future," *Liberation Army Daily* (online), January 17, 2001, p. 17 [in FBIS as "PLA Article Says Space War May Be Future Form of Warfare," January 17, 2001, FBIS document CPP20010117000080].

Li Qingshan (李庆山), *The RMA and High-Tech War* (新军事革命与高技术战争), Beijing: Military Sciences Press, 1995.

Liu Jiangping, Zhu Weitao, and Hu Zili, "A Move Essential for Disintegrating the Enemy's Combined Aerial Attacks: If the Federal Republic of Yugoslavia Attacked NATO's Aircraft Carrier-Led Battle Groups in the Adriatic Sea," *Liberation Army Daily*, August 17, 1999, p. 6 [in FBIS as "Jiefangjun Bao Article on FRY Defense," August, 17 1999, FBIS document FTS19990907001120].

Liu Sunshan, "Military Experts Believe That Coordinate War Is Coming onto the Warfare Stage," *Liberation Army Daily*, June 13, 2001 [in FBIS as "Jiefangjun Bao Article on Accurate All-Weather Attacks Using Satellite Data," June 13, 2001, FBIS document CPP20010613000044].

Liu Weiguo, "The Soft Rib of the High Technology Battlefield: GPS" (现代高技术战场软肋: GPS)," *Liberation Army Daily* (online), July 18, 2001.

Lu Daohai (鲁道海), *Information Operations: Exploring the Seizure of Information Control* (信息作战夺取制信息权的探索), Beijing: Junshi Yiwen Press (军事谊文出版社), 1999.

Lu Linzhi, "Preemptive Strikes Are Crucial in Limited High-Tech Wars," *Jiefangjun bao*, February 7, 1996 [in FBIS as "Preemptive Strikes Endorsed for Limited High-Tech War," February 14, 1996, FBIS document FTS19960214000033].

Mao Zedong, "On Protracted War" (May 1938), in *Selected Works of Mao Zedong*, Vol. II, Beijing: Foreign Languages Press, 1961, pp. 113–194.

McDonald, Joe, "China Parades Accused Taiwanese Spies in Front of Cameras Amid Tensions with Island," Associated Press, January 16, 2004.

"Military Experts Discuss War to Oppose 'Taiwan Independence'" (军事专家谈反台独战争), *People's Daily Online*, November 27, 2003. Online at www1.chinataiwan.org/web/webportal/W2001027/A5390628 .html (as of February 2005).

Minnick, Wendell, "Taiwan-USA Link Up on SIGINT," *Jane's Defense Review*, January 23, 2001.

_____, "Spook Mountain: How US Spies on China," *Asia Times Online*, March 6, 2003. Online at www.atimes.com/atimes/China/EC06Ad03. html (as of February 2005).

_____, "Challenge to Update Taiwan's SIGINT," *Jane's Intelligence Review*, February 1, 2004.

Mulvenon, James, "Party-Army Relations Since the 16th Party Congress: The Battle of the 'Two Centers'?" in Andrew Scobell and Larry Wortzel, eds., *Civil-Military Change in China: Elites, Institutes, and Ideas After the 16th Party Congress*, Carlisle, Pa.: U.S. Army War College, Strategic Studies Institute, 2004, pp. 11–48.

Nan Li, "The PLA's Evolving Campaign Doctrine and Strategies," in James C. Mulvenon and Richard H. Yang, eds., *The People's Liberation Army in the Information Age*, Santa Monica, Calif.: RAND Corporation, CF-145-CAPP/AF, 1999, pp. 146–174.

Nie Yubao (聂玉宝), "Electronic Warfare Methods to Attack Large Enemy Ships (打击海上敌大船艇编队的电子战战法)," in Military Studies Editorial Department, *Research on Our Army's Information Warfare Issues* (我军信息战问题研究), Beijing: National Defense University Press, 1999.

Nu Li, Jiangzhou Li, and Dehui Xu, "Strategies in Information Operations: A Preliminary Discussion," *Military Science,* Vol. 13, No. 2, April 2000, pp. 25–27.

"The Oscar Class: Organizing and Implementing Anti-Ship Operations," *Jianchuan Zhishi,* December 1, 2002, pp. 24–25 [in FBIS as "PRC: Tactics of Oscar-Class Submarine Anti-CVBG Warfare Detailed," December 1, 2002, FBIS document CPP20021203000234].

Pan, Philip P., "China Accelerates Privatization, Continuing Shift from Doctrine," *Washington Post,* November 12, 2003, p. A14.

_____, "China Arrests 43 Alleged Spies; Move Increases Effort to Undermine Taiwanese President," *Washington Post,* December 25, 2003, p. A18.

Pan Xiangting (潘湘庭) and Zhanping Sun (孙占平), eds., *The U.S. Military in Local Wars Under High-Tech Conditions* (高技术条件下美军局部战争), Beijing: PLA Press, 1994.

Peng Guangqian and Youzhi Yao, eds., *The Science of Strategy* (战略学), Beijing: Military Science Press, 2001.

"PLA: Chen Shui-bian Is to Blame If War Breaks Out," *People's Daily Online,* December 3, 2003. Online at http://english.people.com.cn/200312/03/eng20031203_129595.shtml (as of February 2005).

Pomfret, John, "Taiwanese Mistake Led to 3 Spies' Executions," *Washington Post,* February 20, 2000, p. A1.

Pomfret, John, and Philip P. Pan, "Chinese Premier Presses U.S. on Taiwan, Trade," *Washington Post,* November 23, 2003, p. A1.

"Provincial Puzzle," *China Economic Review,* April 2003

Shambaugh, David, *Modernizing China's Military: Progress, Problems, and Prospects,* Berkeley, Calif.: University of California Press, 2002.

Shi Chunmin, "War Is Aimed at the Soft Rib of GPS (战争瞄向GPS '软肋')," *Liberation Army Daily* (online), January 15, 2003. Online at www.pladaily.com.cn/gb/pladaily/2003/01/15/20030115001163_IT.html (as of February 2005).

Singh, Raju Jan, "China's Medium-Term Fiscal Challenges," in International Monetary Fund, *IMF World Economic Outlook: Recessions and Recoveries,* Washington, D.C., April 2002, pp. 36–37.

Solinger, Dorothy, "State and Society in Urban China in the Wake of the 16th Party Congress," *China Quarterly*, Vol. 176, December 2003, pp. 943–959.

"Special Report: Truth or Consequences: China's GDP Numbers," *China Economic Quarterly*, Vol. 8, No. 1, First Quarter 2003, pp. 32–41.

State Statistical Bureau, *China Statistical Yearbook 2002*, Beijing: China Statistics Press, 2002.

Stockholm International Peace Research Institute, SIPRI Facts on International Relations and Security Trends, Military Expenditure Database, http://first.sipri.org (as of February 2005).

Tanner, Murray Scot, "China Rethinks Unrest," *The Washington Quarterly*, Vol. 27, No. 3, Summer 2004a, pp. 137–156.

_____, "Hu Jintao as China's Emerging National Security Leader," in Andrew Scobell and Larry Wortzel, eds., *Civil-Military Change in China: Elites, Institutes, and Ideas After the 16th Party Congress*, Carlisle, Pa.: U.S. Army War College, Strategic Studies Institute, 2004b, pp. 49–76.

"Taiwan Attempts Damage-Control After Alleged Chinese Spy Ring," Agence France-Presse, August 7, 2003.

"Taiwan Detains Woman Over Alleged Spying," *South China Morning Post*, January 30, 2004. Online at http://www.reuters.com/locales/news Article.jsp;:401a497f:84e8183f7e77bb56?type=worldNews&locale=en_I N&storyID=4248298 (as of January 2005).

"Taiwan Spies Visited by Families," Xinhua, January 20, 2004.

"Top PLA Officers Accused of Spying for Taiwan," *Straits Times*, April 16, 2004.

"US to Share Early-Warning Missile Data with Taiwan," Agence France-Presse, October 8, 2002.

U.S. Department of Defense, Office of the Assistant Secretary of Defense (Command, Control, Communications & Intelligence), "Web Site Administration Policies & Procedures," November 25, 1998. Online at www.defenselink.mil/webmasters/policy/dod_web_policy_12071998_wi th_amendments_and_corrections.html (as of February 2005).

_____, *Annual Report on the Military Power of the People's Republic of China*, July 28, 2003.

U.S. National Intelligence Council, *Foreign Missile Developments and the Ballistic Missile Threat Through 2015: Unclassified Summary of a National Intelligence Estimate*, 2001.

Wang Houqing (王厚卿) and Zhang Xingye (张兴业), eds., *Science of Campaigns* (战役学), Beijing: National Defense University Press, 2000.

Wang Hucheng, "The U.S. Military's Soft Ribs and Strategic Weaknesses," Xinhua, July 5, 2000 [in FBIS as "Liaowang on US Military's 'Strategic Weaknesses'," July 5, 2000, FBIS document CPP20000705000081].

Wang Huying (王沪鹰), "The Basic Principles and Campaign Methods of Information Attacks" (信息进攻的基本原则激战法), in Military Studies Editorial Department, *Research on Our Army's Information Warfare Issues*, Beijing: National Defense University Press, 1999, p. 82.

Wei Jincheng, "New Form of People's War," *Jiefangjun bao,* June 25, 1996, p. 6 [in FBIS as "Military Warfare with Chinese Characteristics," June 25, 1996, FBIS document FTS19960625000057].

Wei Yuejiang (魏岳江), "Our Army Explores New Methods for Countering Enemy Over the Horizon Operations" (图文: 我军探究新战法抗强敌远程超视距作战), *Liberation Army Daily* (解放军报) (online), January 27, 2003, www.people.com.cn/GB/junshi/62/20030127/915070.html (as of February 2005).

Wolf, Charles, Jr., K. C. Yeh, Benjamin Zycher, Nicholas Eberstadt, and Sung-Ho Lee, *Fault Lines in China's Economic Terrain*, Santa Monica, Calif.: RAND Corporation, MR-1686-NA/SRF, 2003.

Xie, Andy, "Why High-Speed Growth Won't Solve China's Financial Problems," *SCMP.com*, January 27, 2003.

Xie Yonggao (谢永高), Qin Zizeng (秦子增), and Huang Haibing (黄海兵), "Looking at the Past and Future of Military Aerospace Technology" (军事航天技术的回顾与展望), *China Aerospace* (中国航天), No. 6, 2002. Online at http://www.spacechina.com/index.asp?modelname=zz_nr&recno=55 (as of January 2005).

Xu Yuanxian (徐源先), "Future Basic Methods of Our Army's Information Warfare" (试论未来我军信息战的基本样式), in Military Studies Editorial Department, *Research on Our Army's Information Warfare Issues*, Beijing: National Defense University Press (国防大学出版社), 1999, pp. 29–36.

Yeh, K. C., "China's Economic Growth: Recent Trends and Prospects," in Shuxun Chen and Charles Wolf, Jr., eds., *China, the United States, and the Global Economy*, Santa Monica, Calif.: RAND Corporation, MR-1300-RC, 2001, pp. 69–98.

Zhang Jianhong (张建洪), "Operations to Achieve Campaign Information Control" (夺取战役制信息权作战探要), in Military Studies Editorial Department, *Research on Our Army's Information Warfare Issues*, Beijing: National Defense University Press, 1999 pp. 68–75.

Zhu Rinzhong, "The Theory of GPS and Methods of Countering It," *Junshi Xueshu*, May 1999, pp. 58–59.